**1st EDITION**

# Perspectives on Modern World History

## The Great Depression

**1st EDITION**

# Perspectives on Modern World History

## The Great Depression

David Haugen, Susan Musser,
and Vickey Kalambakal

*Editors*

**GREENHAVEN PRESS**
*A part of Gale, Cengage Learning*

GALE
CENGAGE Learning

Detroit • New York • San Francisco • New Haven, Conn • Waterville, Maine • London

Christine Nasso, *Publisher*
Elizabeth Des Chenes, *Managing Editor*

© 2010 Greenhaven Press, a part of Gale, Cengage Learning.

*For more information, contact:*
Greenhaven Press
27500 Drake Rd.
Farmington Hills, MI 48331-3535
Or you can visit our Internet site at gale.cengage.com

For product information and technology assistance, contact us at
**Gale Customer Support, 1-800-877-4253.**

For permission to use material from this text or product, submit all requests online at
**www.cengage.com/permissions.**

Further permissions questions can be e-mailed to permissionrequest@cengage.com.

Articles in Greenhaven Press anthologies are often edited for length to meet page requirements. In addition, original titles of these works are changed to clearly present the main thesis and to explicitly indicate the author's opinion. Every effort is made to ensure that Greenhaven Press accurately reflects the original intent of the authors. Every effort has been made to trace the owners of copyrighted material.

Cover images © Bettmann/Corbis.

**LIBRARY OF CONGRESS CATALOGING-IN-PUBLICATION DATA**

The Great Depression / David Haugen, Susan Musser, and Vickey Kalambakal, book editors.
  p. cm. -- (Perspectives on modern world history)
  Includes bibliographical references and index.
  ISBN 978-0-7377-4795-9 (hardcover)
1. United States--History--1933-1945--Juvenile literature. 2. United States--History--1919-1933--Juvenile literature. 3. Depressions--1929--United States--Juvenile literature. 4. New Deal, 1933-1939--Juvenile literature. 5. United States--Economic conditions--1918-1945--Juvenile literature. 6. United States--History--1933-1945--Sources--Juvenile literature. 7. United States--History--1919-1933--Sources--Juvenile literature. 8. Depressions--1929--United States--Sources--Juvenile literature. 9. New Deal, 1933-1939--Sources--Juvenile literature. 10. United States--Economic conditions--1918-1945--Sources--Juvenile literature. I. Haugen, David M., 1969- II. Musser, Susan. III. Kalambakal, Vickey.
  E806.G829 2010
  973.917--dc22
                                                                    2009053377

Printed in the United States of America
1 2 3 4 5 6 7 14 13 12 11 10

# CONTENTS

azine editor compares conditions in 1935 to those in 1937 and displays optimism about the revitalization of agriculture in the overworked land through the cooperation of government and local farmers.

**CHAPTER 2**    Controversies Surrounding the Great Depression

Depression did not provide sufficient aid to the people of the United States and thus allowed living conditions at the time to deteriorate.

In 1937, nearly a decade after the stock market crash that triggered the Great Depression, the nation's recovery faltered and the economy entered a recession. President Franklin D. Roosevelt outlines the conditions that caused the setback and argues that financial intervention from the government is necessary to restart economic growth and prosperity.

A Republican senator from Ohio opposes the New Deal legislation, claiming the cost of government intervention has been too high and that such policies have choked the natural recovery of markets. He fears that President Roosevelt has created a welfare state that encourages idleness and dependence.

The chairman of the Tennessee Valley Authority, a government program implemented to provide affordable electricity to residents of the Tennessee Valley region, maintains that government-run utilities can operate alongside private power companies to ensure reasonably priced service to all customers.

global depression if international leaders do not act quickly.

their subsequent deportation as a result of labor surpluses in the bleakest years of the Depression.

# FOREWORD

*"History cannot give us a program for the future, but it can give us a fuller understanding of ourselves, and of our common humanity, so that we can better face the future."*
—*Robert Penn Warren,*
*American poet and novelist*

The history of each nation is punctuated by momentous events that represent turning points for that nation, with an impact felt far beyond its borders. These events—displaying the full range of human capabilities, from violence, greed, and ignorance to heroism, courage, and strength—are nearly always complicated and multifaceted. Any student of history faces the challenge of grasping the many strands that constitute such world-changing events as wars, social movements, and environmental disasters. But understanding these significant historic events can be enhanced by exposure to a variety of perspectives, whether of people involved intimately or of ones observing from a distance of miles or years. Understanding can also be increased by learning about the controversies surrounding such events and exploring hot-button issues from multiple angles. Finally, true understanding of important historic events involves knowledge of the events' human impact—of the ways such events affected people in their everyday lives—all over the world.

Perspectives on Modern World History examines global historic events from the twentieth-century onward by presenting analysis and observation from numerous vantage points. Each volume offers high school, early college level, and general interest readers a thematically

1

arranged anthology of previously published materials that address a major historical event, with an emphasis on international coverage. Each volume opens with background information on the event, then presents the controversies surrounding that event, and concludes with first-person narratives from people who lived through the event or were affected by it. By providing primary sources from the time of the event, as well as relevant commentary surrounding the event, this series can be used to inform debate, help develop critical thinking skills, increase global awareness, and enhance an understanding of international perspectives on history.

Material in each volume is selected from a diverse range of sources, including journals, magazines, newspapers, nonfiction books, personal narratives, speeches, congressional testimony, government documents, pamphlets, organization newsletters, and position papers. Articles taken from these sources are carefully edited and introduced to provide context and background. Each volume of Perspectives on Modern World History includes an array of views on events of global significance. Much of the material comes from international sources and from U.S. sources that provide extensive international coverage.

Each volume in the Perspectives on Modern World History series also includes:

- A full-color **world map**, offering context and geographic perspective.
- An annotated **table of contents** that provides a brief summary of each essay in the volume.
- An **introduction** specific to the volume topic.
- For each viewpoint, a brief **introduction** that has notes about the author and source of the viewpoint, and that provides a summary of its main points.
- Full-color **charts**, **graphs**, **maps**, and other visual representations.

- Informational **sidebars** that explore the lives of key individuals, give background on historical events, or explain scientific or technical concepts.
- A **glossary** that defines key terms, as needed.
- A **chronology** of important dates preceding, during, and immediately following the event.
- A **bibliography** of additional books, periodicals, and Web sites for further research.
- A comprehensive **subject index** that offers access to people, places, and events cited in the text.

Perspectives on Modern World History is designed for a broad spectrum of readers who want to learn more about not only history but also current events, political science, government, international relations, and sociology—students doing research for class assignments or debates, teachers and faculty seeking to supplement course materials, and others wanting to improve their understanding of history. Each volume of Perspectives on Modern World History is designed to illuminate a complicated event, to spark debate, and to show the human perspective behind the world's most significant happenings of recent decades.

# INTRODUCTION

Before the 1930s, any economic downturn could be called a depression or a panic, and such events happened regularly among the global nations. Throughout the nineteenth century, the United States suffered such panics roughly every twenty years, but today, because the crises were not so severe, economists would refer to them as recessions, not depressions. America witnessed many changes in the nineteenth century that destabilized society and the economy—not the least of which was the Civil War, which split the country in two and destroyed the economic strength of the South by ending slavery. Rapid industrialization followed, and this encouraged people to relocate from farms to cities, leaving agriculture behind for factory jobs. The opening of the West, the Gold Rush, and the building of railroads also altered the country's economic character in the post–Civil War decades. In short, America's economy—its production, distribution, and use of goods and services—changed in every conceivable way. Such upheavals brought progress and a higher standard of living, but they also contributed to depressions in 1819, 1837, 1857, 1873, 1893, and 1907, as speculation, fraud, deflation, and other factors followed the boom and bust of markets that capitalized on gold fever, warfare, and similar historic events shaping an expanding nation. Each of these depressions seemed worse than the previous one, and all generated grim statistics reflecting rising unemployment, home foreclosures, shuttered businesses, and industrial slowdowns.

The Great Depression of the 1930s was worse than any of its nineteenth- and early-twentieth-century predecessors, however. Its impact was so severe because every aspect of the economy felt the weight of the collapse. While previous depressions were typically centered on slowdowns in one specific industry—such as railroads in the panic of 1873—or on policies that led to increased inflation, the Great Depression was characterized by the complete breakdown of the investor market, the industrial sector, and the banking arena. The collapse was so great that even today, no downturn, no matter how dire, has merited the label "depression."

Most experts agree that the Great Depression's roots go back to a period well before the advent of the First World War, when the United States became the world's richest country with a GNP (gross national product) five times greater than the GNPs of most European countries. America was experiencing tremendous economic growth as it expanded to fill its new western and southern borders. With such growth came economic influence through rising exports and imports, ensuring that any ripple in the U.S. markets would be felt across the globe.

America's economy kept growing through World War I as well. Physically untouched by the devastation that plagued Europe, American production lines were in full swing to furnish others nations with what they needed to rebuild after the war ended in 1918. To pay for the war and reconstruction, many European nations went off the gold standard—that is, they could no longer afford to back their currency with gold. The lack of a gold standard led to inflation after the war as governments printed more money to finance rebuilding. British economist Lionel Robbins noted in his 1934 book *The Great Depression*, "Whether or not it be welcomed as a solution for certain very pressing domestic problems, no really impartial observer of world events can do other than regard the abandonment of the Gold Standard by Great Britain as a catastrophe of the first order of magnitude." Many countries also set tariffs to protect their own manufacturers and keep wages high. By 1921, European markets had recovered enough that U.S. industry began to feel competition from cheap European goods. In that year and the next, the U.S. government passed high tariffs to strengthen internal demand for American-made products.

Throughout the 1920s, American industry continued to prosper, and U.S. investors were eager to profit from the growth. A stock market boom tempted many Americans—from large financiers to small-time speculators—to put money into stocks. Most stocks could be bought "on margin," meaning that the investor only had to pay a fraction of the stock price up front, then owe the rest to trading houses that put up the remainder. By 1929, millions of Americans were buying stocks, but much of the value was tied to the hope that the stocks could be quickly sold so that investors could pay off their margin debt and make a profit. Seven billion dollars of the money invested in the market was borrowed from trading houses, covering stocks bought on margin. If stock prices fell across the board, the brokers simply could not cover the losses.

Unfortunately, most stocks were over-valued from the outset. From 1925 on, companies had been producing more goods than they could sell, but speculators were willing to overlook this reality in the mad dash to invest in just about anything. Even though sales dropped in the second half of the decade, companies kept producing, believing sales would rise again. The one exception was agriculture; farmers had never recovered from a slump after World War I ended. But other industries—steel foundries, auto manufacturers, furniture and appliance makers, and the like—simply churned out more products, and to entice consumers to pick up the slack, businesses began offering credit lines. Thus, many families went into debt to buy new cars and furnishings in the post-war boom years. American historian David E. Kyvig notes in his book *Daily Life in the United States*

*1920–1940: How Americans Lived through the Roaring Twenties and the Great Depression* that in 1921, only two years after General Motors introduced its own credit company, "half of all automobile buyers were entering into credit purchase agreements; by 1926 the figure reached three-fourths."

In the late 1920s, however, consumer demand just could not keep pace with supply. Fewer homes were being built, for example, but most economists of the time did not interpret such declines as symptoms of economic trouble. Influential voices of the economy such as E.H.H. Simmons, president of the New York Stock Exchange, denied the possibility of a coming downturn. In January 1928 he stated, "I cannot help but raise a dissenting voice to statements that we are living in a fool's paradise, and that prosperity in this country must necessarily diminish and recede in the near future." More significantly, the government was not helping to correct the downturns. Under the post-war presidencies of Warren G. Harding and Calvin Coolidge, the Federal Reserve was printing more money, driving interest rates down. When demand for goods cooled late in the decade, the government contracted the money supply. With more money out of circulation, credit dried up, and investors finally recognized that the Roaring Twenties were about to end.

Large financiers who wanted to secure their holding dumped stocks in order to invest in gold and bonds. With big-time investors flooding markets with stocks, the values of everyone's shares began to drop. Many people rushed to sell their stocks before their margins were called; others were forced to let go of the investments because they could not pay what was owed to the trading houses. Beginning in September 1929, the market experienced heavy trading until its final collapse in late October when millions of shares traded hands in less than a week. Even at this lowest ebb, some financiers and economists thought the market would rebound now that the fair-weather investors had departed. As 1930 began, U.S. secretary of the treasury Andrew W. Mellon remained hopeful about the country's economic future proclaiming, "I see nothing . . . in the present situation that is either menacing or warrants pessimism . . . I have every confidence that there will be a revival of activity in the spring and that during the coming year, the country will make steady progress." It was not to be. Several factors conspired to ensure that the recession that followed the stock market collapse would turn into a full-blown depression of profound proportions. What influence each of these factors had on the fate of the economy, however, has been debated since the days following the October debacle on Wall Street.

In 1932, chief counsel to the U.S. Senate Ferdinand Pecora led congressional hearings to discover why the stock market had crashed. Pecora's report—all twelve thousand pages of it—pointed to the lack of regulation on Wall Street and unsound banking practices. Once these findings were made public, Americans were agreeable to the establishment of watchdog agencies like the Securities and Exchange Commission and the Federal Depository Insurance Corporation, which ensured government involvement in the stock market and the banking industry. Although such intervention was unprecedented, many Americans at the time believed that government oversight of Wall Street—that Pecora excoriated for perpetuating abuses and fraud—was just punishment for the supposedly unscrupulous financiers who brought the nation to its knees. However, since the Depression, economists and historians have painted the stock market collapse as a result, not a cause, of a long-brewing financial crisis.

Other analysts argue that the stock market crash alone did not account for the depth and breadth of the crisis or for the fact that that it would last for a decade in America. The late Nobel Prize–winning economist

Milton Friedman and his followers—including Ben Bernanke, the current head of the Federal Reserve—believe that the wrongheaded policies of the Federal Reserve in 1929 plunged the nation from stock-market-induced recession into the Great Depression. In a 2000 interview, Friedman stated, "We had repeated recessions over hundreds of years, but what converted [the 1929 one] into a major depression was bad monetary policy." If the Federal Reserve had acted to increase the monetary supply in the critical months between October 1929 and the beginning of 1932, Friedman asserted, it might have forestalled a depression. However, because the Federal Reserve allowed the available money to decline by a third, credit dried up and interest rates rose, compelling most people to hoard their cash instead of injecting it back into the economy.

Another common scapegoat blamed for aggravating the situation is Herbert Hoover, the U.S. president in office during the early years of the Depression. Though many historians have often portrayed Hoover as maintaining hands-off, "laissez-faire" policies toward the economy, thus allowing the problems to worsen, some modern researchers have suggested that Hoover may have done just the opposite. University of California macroeconomist Lee Ohanian claims that Hoover's pro-labor stance exacerbated the initial stock market recession by not permitting industry to cut worker pay in response to falling commodity prices. "By keeping industrial wages too high," Ohanian writes, "Hoover sharply depressed employment beyond where it otherwise would have been, and that act drove down the overall gross national product. His policy was the single most important event in precipitating the Great Depression." Other revisionist historians have similarly argued that Hoover's high-tariff policies—enacted to fulfill a campaign promise to help America's farmers compete with foreign imports—were designed to help the nation's workers but unintentionally squeezed exports when U.S. trading partners enacted high tariffs in retaliation. These historians insist that, with declining imports and exports, America's economic stability was compromised and the Depression unnecessarily protracted.

Causation aside, what the deepening Depression did to Americans can be tracked through statistics, photos, newspaper stories, and memoirs. Confidence sagged, and the economy did not rebound under Hoover's administration. Then in 1930, a drought began in the Great Plains that lasted years. Farming, which was still a major part of the financial stability of the nation, was disrupted in parts of five states. The resulting Dust Bowl—the worst ecological disaster the U.S. has ever suffered—was characterized by dust storms composed of precious topsoil loosened by lack of water and years of poor farming methods. The dust swept the plains, burying farms; some of the storms, hundreds of miles wide, blew soil all the way to the East Coast. The drought drove more than 2.5 million people from the Great Plains, swelling the ranks of the unemployed in other areas. With the nation's agricultural base damaged and the industrial centers unable to pay more hands, America's unemployment rate reached nearly 25 percent by 1933. Around 11,385,000 Americans waited through the country's darkest time to find both work and a sense of hope that prosperity would return.

For many Americans, the inauguration of President Franklin Delano Roosevelt in 1933 seemed to herald needed change. His New Deal policy package shored up sound banks, stabilized agriculture and commodity prices, and started public works programs that put thousands of Americans to work. The programs entailed massive government spending, and though their effectiveness in ending the Depression is debated to this day, they gave the feeling that the government was actively working toward a solution to the problems of unemployment and the plummeting value of goods. Still, the Great Depression would drag on for more than half a decade as New Deal plans were implemented, altered, and even scrapped in an attempt to get America working again. In recent years, historians and economists have begun to question whether the New Deal policies actually played a role in ending the Depression. In the introduction to American historian Burton W. Folsom, Jr.'s book critiquing FDR's New Deal, *New Deal or Raw Deal? How FDR's Economic Legacy Has Damaged America, Wall Street Journal* senior economics writer Stephen Moore contends, "The most damning indictment of FDR's New Deal agenda is that it did not do what it set out to do: end the Great Depression." While scholars continue to debate the success of the New Deal, most historians agree that the coming of World War II in 1939 changed the economic fortunes of the nation in ways that Roosevelt's programs could not. Suddenly the demand for war material invigorated the country's industrial sector, and the demand for food in Europe and Asia put farming back on track. When America finally entered the war, unemployment rates had dropped below 10 percent. The nation was accruing a large national debt in paying for war, but this compromise seemed acceptable—at least in the short term—for ensuring that the Great Depression was a thing of the past.

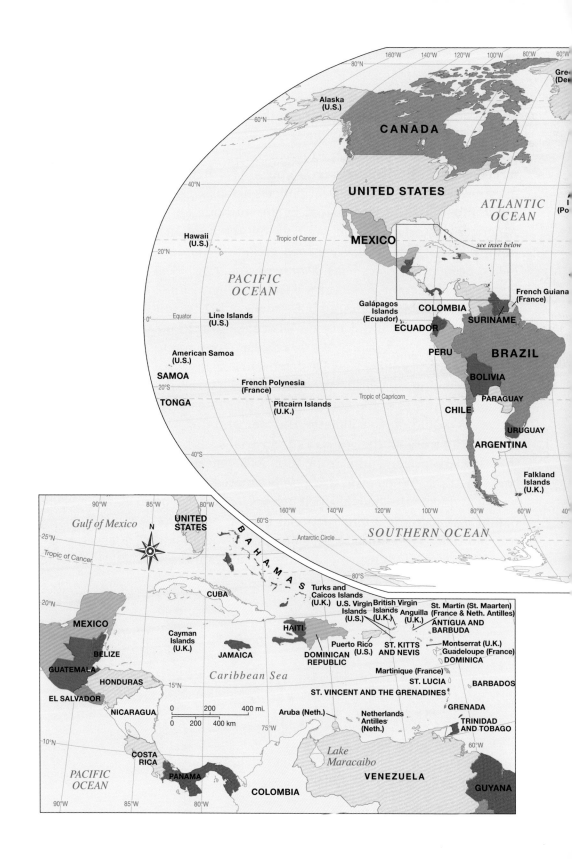

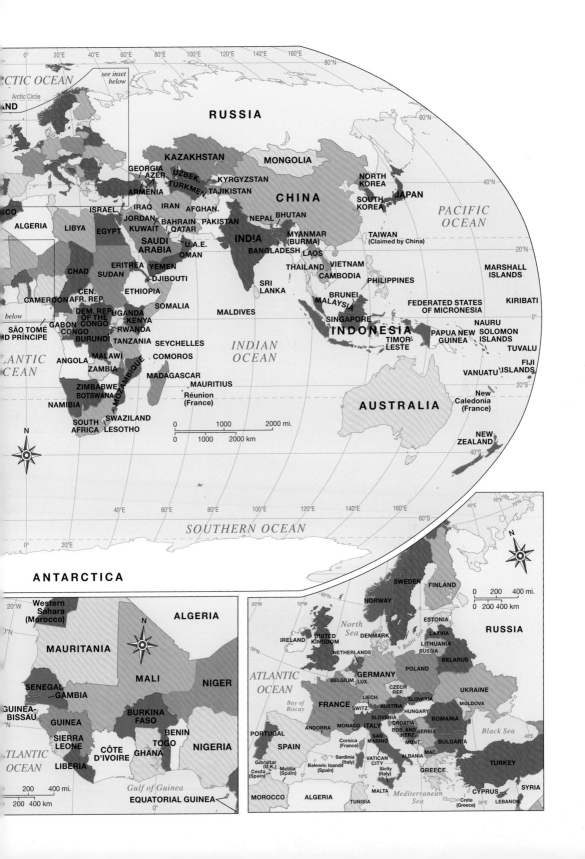

# CHAPTER 1

# Historical Background
# on the Great Depression

# The Great Depression: An Overview

## Kelly King Howes

Following World War I, the United States experienced a decade of prosperity and growth that lasted until the stock market crash of 1929, which preceded the Great Depression. In the following viewpoint, Kelly King Howes provides an overview of the events leading up to the crash and the decade that followed. Howes maintains that the stock market crash joined a variety of factors, from falling agricultural prices and wages to exorbitant European war debt, to cause the financial crisis. The response of President Herbert Hoover, Howes contends, was insufficient to combat the poverty and suffering of the millions of Americans who lost their jobs and were unable to purchase basic necessities. She goes on to assert that dissatisfaction with the government's handling of the crisis opened the door for Franklin D. Roosevelt to win the 1932 presidential election and gave him the leverage needed to implement a series of policies known as the New Deal. Kelly King Howes is an American author who has

Photo on previous page: The market crash on October 29, 1929, which preceded the Great Depression, had its start at the New York Stock Exchange. (**AP Images.**)

**SOURCE.** Kelly King Howes, *Roaring Twenties: Almanac and Primary Sources.* Detroit, MI: U-X-L, 2006. © 2006 Gale, a part of Cengage Learning Inc. Reproduced by permission of Gale, a part of Cengage Learning.

written books on late-nineteenth- and early-twentieth-century American history.

T hroughout the 1920s a pro-business atmosphere had dominated the United States, and the economy had flourished, with companies expanding, foreign trade thriving, and the stock market on the rise. When President Herbert Hoover (1874–1964; served 1929–1933) took office in early 1929, he declared in his inaugural address, "I have no fears for the future of our country. It is bright with hope." By the end of the year, these words would ring hollow.

But Hoover was not the only one who felt optimistic. Others also predicted a continuation of business as usual. Alfred Sloan (1875–1966), president of General Motors, made his own pronouncement, as quoted in [American journalist] Nathan Miller's *New World Coming: The 1920s and the Making of Modern America*: "Personally, I believe it is going to be a very good year—I don't see how it could be otherwise."

## A Get-Rich-Quick Mentality

Before the 1920s, few ordinary U.S. citizens had invested in the stock market, which was considered a pursuit for the wealthy. But the decade brought not only extra cash to many but also a get-rich-quick mentality, along with a close alliance between business and government that made all kinds of business activities seem more acceptable. Many more people, including some of modest income, were buying and selling stocks. There were not as many, though, as some accounts of the 1920s have suggested: of a total U.S. population of 120 million, only about 1.5 million were involved with

> The prices of stocks were far higher than their real value and out of proportion to the profit-making ability of the companies.

the stock market. More significant was the way that the stock boom became a popular, well-received part of U.S. culture.

When an investor buys stock (also called shares) in a company, he or she provides it with money with which to operate. If the company does well and makes a profit, the investor receives a share of that money in the form of a dividend, and the stock he owns becomes more valuable. He can sell it for more than the purchase price. A rise in the price of a stock means that it has become more valuable, usually because the company has been successful or seems promising. If the stock price goes down, however, the investor may lose money if he sells (he may, of course, choose to hold on to the stock in the hope that its value will rise again). Many of the investors of the 1920s were indulging in speculation, which means that they were buying and selling stocks quickly to make fast profits.

Some of the people who were now investing in the stock market used their own savings, while others bought stocks through a kind of credit system called "on the margin." This meant that they paid a small amount, usually about 10 percent, of the price of the stock while the stockbroker (a person who is authorized to conduct stock sales) paid the rest. If stock prices rose, the investor could pay back the debt while also making a profit. If prices fell, however, he or she would have to pay back the full amount to the stockbroker right away. By late 1929 broker loans totaled close to $7 billion.

The prospect of easy money and instant wealth had great appeal during the 1920s. By the end of the decade, the New York Stock Exchange—the center for stock trading, located on Wall Street in New York City—was trading six to seven million shares (or stocks) per day, compared to a more normal rate of three to four million. The prices of stocks were far higher than their real value and out of proportion to the profit-making ability of the companies. Yet people continued to invest enthusiasti-

cally, believing that prices could rise indefinitely to make them richer and richer.

## Warning Signs of the Coming Crisis

Even as stock prices and investor enthusiasm were rising at a frantic pace, there were indications that not all was well with the economy. According to Miller, "Despite the continuation of the era of wonderful nonsense, cracks in the nation's economic foundation were evident to those who looked closely."

Ever since the end of World War I, when the demand for farm products that the European conflict had brought came to an end, farmers had been suffering from hard times. There was a huge oversupply of food in the United States, and prices were dropping dramatically. For example, a bushel of wheat that had cost $2.57 in 1920 cost only $1.00 a year later. As the decade progressed, wheat prices fell even more, and the coal mining and textile (cloth) industries were also in trouble. Construction on new houses slowed drastically; in the short period between 1928 and 1929, the construction industry declined by $1 billion.

Wages were also in decline, which meant that more and more people were unable to keep up with their former pace of consumerism (the preoccupation with acquiring goods that had dominated much of the decade). Radios and other items stayed on store shelves, and cars gathered dust on dealership lots, while new production slowed down. Unemployment was on the rise, an especially troubling sign during a decade in which most people had been able to find work. In Europe, changes in monetary policies and political unrest created instability that sent ripples across the sea to the United States.

A few sharp observers were calling attention to these trends, such as financial adviser Roger Babson, who predicted, as quoted in Miller's book, that "sooner or later a crash is coming." A few big investors, including the very

Photo on previous page: His fortune lost in the 1929 stock market crash, former millionaire "Champagne Fred" Bell sells apples on a San Francisco street in 1931. (AP Images.)

wealthy Joseph Kennedy (1888–1969), father of future president John F. Kennedy (1917–1963; served 1960–1963), started selling off stocks. Even President Hoover knew the danger of the kind of out-of-control speculation that was taking place. His belief that government should allow business to manage its own affairs as much as possible, however, was so strong that he did little to interfere.

## The Stock Market Crash

From September to October of 1929, the stock market rose to incredible heights. The widespread belief that things could continue this way came to a screeching halt on October 24, a day that would always be known as Black Thursday. The day before, stock trading had been especially heavy. But even before the bell that traditionally opened the New York Stock Exchange stopped ringing that Thursday morning, prices began to fall with stunning swiftness. The ticker tape (the ribbon-like paper in the telegraphic machine that printed information about stock prices) could not keep up with the pace of transactions as traders frantically bought and sold.

> In only a few hours, stocks had lost about $10 million in value.

Brokers began calling in their loans, and investors who had bought on the margin could not pay back their debts. Disaster, or the fear that disaster was just around the corner, was in the air. Crowds gathered in New York City's financial district, and extra police were sent in to control them. Rumors flew, especially those claiming that bankrupt investors and desperate brokers were killing themselves by jumping off buildings. In fact, a workman seen on top of a Wall Street building was wrongly assumed to be on the verge of suicide.

A measure of calm was introduced in the early afternoon, when a group of prominent bankers pooled their resources and bought $40 million worth of blue-chip shares (reliably valuable shares in leading companies like General Motors and U.S. Steel). This helped to restore people's confidence in the market and to reduce the panic somewhat. The relief proved short-lived, though. On the following Tuesday, October 29, Black Tuesday, came an even worse crash. Orders to sell stocks flooded the stock market, but hardly anyone was buying. Not even the blue-chip stocks were being bought.

The Federal Reserve (the government agency that makes rules for the banking industry) called a hasty meeting but could not decide what to do. In only a few hours, stocks had lost about $10 million in value. More than sixteen million shares were sold during the day. Chaos reigned in and around the New York Stock Exchange as well as in brokers' offices and banks across the country. Banks had lent speculators money that they had in turn borrowed from corporations. The corporations were now demanding that the banks repay their loans, and the banks were quickly running out of the funds needed to do so. Those funds included the savings that people had entrusted to the banks, which were now being wiped out.

## Numerous Factors Caused the Depression

Despite the drama, surprise, and shock of the October crash, the idea that it caused an instant plunge into the harsh conditions of the Great Depression is faulty. For a few months it was not at all clear how much impact the disaster would have on the wider economy. Meanwhile, financial and government leaders tried to figure out what to do. President Hoover called for calm and then stuck to his usual policy of politely requesting cooperation and voluntary action from the business world. He asked manufacturers to cut into their profits before making pay cuts or trimming jobs, and he urged state and local governments to start public works projects (such as the

| | UNEMPLOYMENT, GDP, AND FEDERAL SPENDING | | |
|---|---|---|---|
| Year | Unemployment Rate | Real GDP (in billions of dollars) | Federal Spending (in millions of dollars) |
| 1929 | 3.2% | $951.7 | $3,127 |
| 1930 | 8.9% | $862.1 | $3,320 |
| 1931 | 16.3% | $788.8 | $3,577 |
| 1932 | 24.1% | $682.9 | $4,659 |
| 1933 | 25.2% | $668.6 | $4,598 |
| 1934 | 22.0% | $719.8 | $6,541 |
| 1935 | 20.3% | $778.2 | $6,412 |
| 1936 | 17.0% | $888.2 | $8,228 |
| 1937 | 14.3% | $932.5 | $7,580 |
| 1938 | 19.1% | $890.8 | $6,840 |

Taken from: Fed Bank St. Louis, "The Great Depression."

building of roads and parks) to put people to work. In a remark often attributed to Hoover, Vice President Charles Curtis (1860–1936), as quoted in Miller, declared that "Prosperity is just around the corner."

By the spring of 1930, however, there were more bad signs. A full-fledged economic depression had begun as wages were cut, workers were laid off from their jobs, and factories closed. This led to a drop in consumer spending. Farm prices fell, and a terrible drought in the midwestern and southern states ruined crops and livelihoods. More and more banks closed, with depositors losing all of their savings. By the end of the year, sixteen hundred banks had closed. According to Frederick Lewis Allen[1] in his [1931] book *Only Yesterday: An Informal History of the 1920s*, "The grocer, the window-cleaner, and the seamstress had lost their capital. In every town there were families which had suddenly dropped from showy affluence into debt."

Following a slight, temporary improvement in the economy in early 1931, the economic decline continued. Influences from abroad were also having an impact. The 1930 passage of the Hawley-Smoot Tariff (a tax that foreign countries had to pay on goods they wanted to sell in the United States) led to a decline in products coming into the country, while the demand for U.S. goods and food overseas also slowed. The European economies were in trouble too. In fact they had been since the end of World War I. The European countries had borrowed money from the United States to pay for the war effort, but now they could not pay back those loans. These factors made the U.S. economic situation even worse. Although Hoover put most of the blame for the nation's troubles on outside influences, most analysts cite the weak links in the U.S. economy itself as the main cause.

> " Even with so many suffering, [Herbert] Hoover continued to do little to help. "

## The Devastating Impact of the Depression

As the Depression continued, it took a heavy toll on every aspect of the nation's life. Before it was over, unemployment would reach as high as seventeen million, or more than one-quarter of the workforce; in some places, it would hit especially hard (such as Toledo, Ohio, where 80 percent were out of work). The overall national income would be slashed in half.

Worst of all, perhaps, was the impact of the Depression at the most personal level. Previously prosperous or comfortably well-off families were now broke. Men in business suits sold apples from carts on street corners. In contrast to the consumerism practiced during the Roaring Twenties, people had to save their pennies and do without not only luxuries, but also necessities.

Lost-looking, weary faces were seen on the bread-lines and in the soup kitchens (set up to provide the poor with food) in every city, and thousands of men and boys, as well as a few women, hopped freight trains to look for work or simply escape from the shame and harsh realities they faced at home. Farmers who were unable to pay back their debts watched their land, houses, and possessions being auctioned off.

Despite some gains made in the first decades of the twentieth century, African Americans had always been subject to discrimination and had always been at the bottom level of society. They suffered even more now. Their unemployment rate was four to six times higher than that of whites, as even the least desirable jobs were now often taken by white people.

Even with so many suffering, Hoover continued to do little to help. The United States did not yet have unemployment insurance, which provides income to those laid off from their jobs, and the president did not approve of giving direct aid to people who were out of work. He did, however, increase spending on public works, and he directed the Federal Farm Board to buy and store surplus food from farmers in order to keep prices stable. Hoover also gave a certain amount of government money to endangered banks, railroads, and insurance companies. He was hesitant, though, to put too much money into these efforts or to give them much time to take effect.

## The American People Voted for Change

Members of the Democratic Party were in a relatively happy mood as they gathered in Chicago in June 1932 to choose a candidate for the November presidential election. After a whole decade of Republican dominance of the U.S. government, the

> In accepting the nomination of his party, [Franklin D.] Roosevelt said, 'I pledge you, I pledge myself to a new deal for the American people.'

Democrats now seemed to stand a very good chance of gaining power. They knew that the people of the United States were eager for change, and that much of the blame for the nation's woes was being cast on Hoover and his fellow Republicans.

Nine candidates vied for the nomination, which was eventually won by New York governor Franklin Delano Roosevelt (1882–1945; served 1933–1945). He was a dynamic person who was widely respected for having used some effective measures to deal with the Depression in his own state. In accepting the nomination of his party, Roosevelt said, "I pledge you, I pledge myself to a new deal for the American people." (The phrase "new deal" would later be used as the name of the economic program that Roosevelt would put in place.) During the campaign, the Democrats avoided the issues that had divided people in previous years, especially that of Prohibition, the controversial ban on alcoholic beverages that had gone into effect at the beginning of the 1920s, and focused on the economy.

That summer, Hoover's reputation was damaged even more by his harsh treatment of World War I veterans who had marched to Washington, D.C., to demand early payment of a bonus promised for 1945. As many as twenty thousand men had gathered in the nation's capital. After Congress turned down their request, most of them left, but Hoover sent in the army to chase out the rest. There were many injuries, and two of the veterans were killed, creating much bad feeling.

The November 1932 election resulted in a resounding victory for Roosevelt. At his inauguration, broadcast into an estimated sixty million U.S. homes by radio, the new president assured U.S. citizens that "the only thing we have to fear is fear itself." He promised that his New Deal plan would put the nation back on track through such measures as public works projects for the unemployed, the stimulation of farm prices, loans to prevent foreclosures (when banks take possession of property due to failure to repay the debt), and new regulations to control banking and credit practices. The 1935 Social Security Act would ensure income for retired or disabled workers.

## Note

1. Frederick Lewis Allen was a U.S. historian and magazine editor who lived during the first half of the twentieth century.

# The New Deal: An Overview

## Dana Magill

After his election in 1932, Franklin D. Roosevelt and his presidential administration implemented a series of policies collectively termed the New Deal. In the following viewpoint, Dana Magill outlines some of the major policies of Roosevelt's New Deal, dividing the policies into three categories—relief, recovery, and reform. Magill describes how these various government programs provided immediate aid in the form of government handouts and federal work programs; economic restoration through government subsidies and the temporary allowance of price-fixing; and measures to prevent future financial crises of that scale with the formation of agencies such as the Securities and Exchange Commission and the Federal Deposit Insurance Company. Magill also discusses the creation of the Tennessee Valley Authority, a federal utilities program that she explains did not fit into any of these three categories yet related strongly to Roosevelt's belief that government could best serve the interests of the people by reforming certain industries. Dana Magill

**SOURCE.** Dana Magill, *Encyclopedia of Politics, Vol. 1: The Left.* Thousand Oaks, CA: Sage Reference, 2005. Copyright © 2005 by Sage Publications, Inc. All rights reserved. Used with permission of Sage Publications, conveyed through Copyright Clearance Center, Inc.

is a professor of history at Stephen F. Austin State University in Texas. She specializes in women's history and American history.

The New Deal refers collectively to the domestic programs that President Franklin D. Roosevelt and his administration enacted in response to the Great Depression. The term is applied to the period of history from 1933, when Roosevelt's term in office began, until the onset of World War II in 1939.

New Deal programs involved a tremendous amount of federal legislation, government programs, bureaus, agencies, and commissions. Many of these programs had overlapping functions and jurisdictions, some of which had similar names. New Deal programs were often referred to by an alphabetical abbreviation, thus leading to the remark that an "alphabet soup" had been created. The extensive and multifaceted nature of the New Deal programs represent Roosevelt's willingness to utilize many approaches and to try anything that he thought might work. He was not, as was his predecessor Herbert Hoover, bound by a conviction that it was not the role of the government to involve itself in the economy. While Hoover opposed direct government aid to individuals in distress, Roosevelt felt that intervention was necessary. At one point in his presidency, he commanded one of his aides: "I don't care how you do it. Feed them, damn it, feed them."

Roosevelt was elected president in November 1932, to the first of four terms. By March 1933, 13 million people were unemployed, and almost every bank had

> The Roosevelt administration felt people would have more self-respect if they worked for a living and preferred establishing federal projects in which a person might be employed . . . and paid wages.

closed. In his first 100 days in office, he proposed and Congress enacted numerous programs to bring recovery to business and agriculture, relief to the unemployed and to those in danger of losing farms and homes, and reform programs that attempted to prevent another great depression from occurring and to cushion the economic effect in case one did. In an effort to organize New Deal programs clearly, historians usually divide them into three main groups: relief, recovery, and reform.

## Programs that Provided Immediate Relief

Relief programs were designed to relieve economic suffering immediately by feeding those who were on the verge of starvation and by putting people back to work—working for the government if necessary. It included the Federal Emergency Relief Administration (FERA). This agency provided direct government aid, an outright government handout, to individuals in need. The Roosevelt administration felt people would have more self-respect if they worked for a living and preferred establishing federal projects in which a person might be employed by the government and paid wages or a salary. The program put people to work for the government as soon as possible by doing something that would benefit society. But the FERA was considered only a temporary measure.

People were put to work on a more permanent basis through other programs such as the Public Works Administration (PWA). Under this program, large sums of money were appropriated to be spent on giant public work projects such as building dams or large public buildings. The unemployed hired for such projects were paid by the government. Next, the Works Progress Administration (WPA) was similar in name and in concept to the PWA and employed people in a variety of public service tasks. Generally, WPA projects were not as large as PWA projects. For instance, WPA projects built college buildings while the PWA built great dams. Furthermore, WPA projects were much more varied than PWA. For example, WPA projects employed artists to paint pictures in post offices, historians to write history books, and actors to put on plays for the public. Many public buildings in use today were originally built as WPA projects. Finally, the National Youth Administration (NYA) and the Civilian Conservation Corps (CCC) employed young people in some kind of public service capacity.

> The government hoped to reach a point in which their intervention would be eliminated. This point never came.

## Programs for Long-Term Economic Recovery

Recovery programs were designed to return the economy to a normal, healthy state. Efforts were made to get business, labor, and agriculture back to a profitable basis. The first of these programs included the National Recovery Administration (NRA) as an effort to aid business and labor. Under the NRA, business and industrial firms dealing in the same area (for example, the steel industry as a whole, or the shoe manufacturing industry as a whole) were encouraged to cooperatively set certain prices that they might charge for their goods and still make a profit. Certainly, such price-fixing was a violation of the free-market concept and of anti-trust laws [laws to ensure competition in the marketplace and to protect consumers] passed in the Progressive period.[1] Nonetheless, this became allowable in the early part of the New Deal through justification that emergency measures were needed. Participating firms displayed a blue eagle, the symbol of the NRA, at their business locations. Later on, the price-fixing aspect of the New Deal was terminated.

The Agriculture Adjustment Administration (AAA) also functioned as a recovery program. This program was designed to help agriculture become profitable again. Roosevelt recognized overproduction as a serious problem and felt that encouraging farmers to decrease their production would be the solution. To encourage them to do so, the government paid farmers a subsidy to reduce production, a practice that exists today. . . . The government hoped to reach a point in which their intervention would be eliminated. This point never came. . . .

## Reform Measures to Prevent Another Great Depression

Finally, Roosevelt and his administration devised several reform programs. The first program, the Securities Exchange Commission (SEC), still exists today. It was established to regulate the sale of securities such as stocks and bonds. The program hoped to insure responsible dealings and the prevention of irresponsible practices that brought the stock market crashing down in the 1920s. The Federal Deposit Insurance Corporation (FDIC), also in existence today, is a government corporation created to insure bank deposits up to a designated amount. Should a bank fail, the government backs the deposits. This act seeks to prevent another failure of banks as happened in the Great Depression. Banks today often have signs on the door, "Member F.D.I.C." Finally, and perhaps the most well known program of the New Deal, Social Security began under Roosevelt. Social Security includes three parts: old age pension, unemployment insurance, and welfare. Old age pensions (commonly called Social Security today though the whole program is collectively called Social Security) provide a compulsory pension for elderly people over a certain age. Unemployment insurance provides income for those who have become unemployed with some limitations. Welfare payments are designated for individuals who, for various reasons, are unable to work or support themselves or their family at a minimum living standard.

Moses Soyer's 1935 painting *Artists on WPA* shows the painter's colleagues at work on portable murals. (MPI/Getty Images.)

## Providing Cheap Power to Rural Areas

Another part of the New Deal that does not easily fit into relief, reform, or recovery, is the Tennessee Valley Authority (TVA). During the New Deal, the government undertook a great project to develop and economically rehabilitate the valley of the Tennessee River. The river was harnessed by dams, and experts were sent in to help farmers learn better methods of agriculture in a great effort to transform the economy of the region from a depressed area to a thriving one. Under the TVA, dams produced electricity and the government sold, and still sells, the electricity to consumers at a cheaper rate than they could get it from private power companies. Those in the Tennessee area pay much cheaper electric rates today. New Deal supporters dreamed of doing the same thing in other river valleys such as the Missouri, Mississippi, Columbia, and Arkansas, but the TVA is the only one that was launched before World War II. After the war, public opinion did not favor more of these experiments. Thus, the TVA is the only one of its kind and represents a unique experiment in American history.

> The New Deal marked a critical departure in the governing principles, institutional arrangements, and policies that shaped modern American political life.

## A New Role for the U.S. Government

By 1939, the New Deal had run its course. In the short term, New Deal programs helped improve the lives of people suffering from the events of the Depression. In the long run, New Deal programs set a precedent for the federal government to play a key role in the economic and social affairs of the nation. Roosevelt's New Deal emphasized security rather than the redistribution of wealth, and the programs marked the United States government's first significant, direct investment in the everyday lives of Americans.

In establishing the New Deal, Roosevelt offered an alternative vision by presenting the government as an instrument of reform. In his view, the government represented a new order, one founded on hope rather than fear, and opportunity rather than dependence. The New Deal marked a critical departure in the governing principles, institutional arrangements, and policies that shaped modern American political life. Roosevelt reconstructed the definitions of American political parties and transformed the perception of the duty of the government as viewed by the people well beyond his years in office. As the successor of the Progressive Era and precursor to the

Great Society, the New Deal stressed structural change rather than economic recovery; therefore, the birth of New Deal liberalism was a defining moment in the 20th century.

Although the New Deal was perceived at the time as a movement to the left in American politics, most of the permanent reforms and agencies established during the period were quite centrist from the perspective of social-democratic regimes in Europe. The National Recovery Administration had been built on an Associative State concept, in which code authorities would regulate the economy in the national interest. However, with the Supreme Court ruling that the code authorities represented unwarranted delegation of the power to legislate to administrative agencies in the *Schechter* case,[2] that experiment ended.

The wide variety of other agencies, ranging from the TVA with its direct government financing of electrical power to provide a yardstick for power pricing and some development of rural Appalachia, to simple regulatory bodies, did not represent a challenge to the private enterprise, capitalist structure of American society. Indeed, by ameliorating some of the worst conditions of the Great Depression, the New Deal could be said to have preserved the American political economy from a more revolutionary approach.

## Notes

1. A historical era in the United States beginning in 1890 and lasting through the 1920s, marked by economic, political, and social reform.
2. The 1935 Supreme Court case *Schechter Poultry Corp. v. United States* dealt with federal regulation of the poultry industry.

# Industrial Growth Fosters American Prosperity

## Julius H. Barnes

Following the conclusion of World War I, during the decade known as the "Roaring Twenties," the United States experienced dramatic industrial growth and widespread prosperity. In April 1929, just months before the October 1929 stock market crash that signaled the onset of the Great Depression, Julius H. Barnes, then chairman of the Chamber of Commerce of the United States, spoke about the role of industry in improving the lives of Americans and fostering increased wealth nationwide. In that address, he provided specific examples of newly developed products, such as cars, radios, and refrigerators, that raised the U.S. standard of living, and he discussed the ways in which investment in the stock market allowed all U.S. citizens the opportunity to capitalize on the wealth generated by industry. During his tenure as chairman of the U.S. Chamber of Commerce from 1922 through the early 1930s, Julius H. Barnes

**SOURCE.** Julius H. Barnes, Address before the Seventeenth Annual Meeting of the Chamber of Commerce of the United States, Washington, DC: U.S. Chamber of Commerce, 1929.

wrote and spoke extensively about the sweeping changes occurring in the U.S. economy. His brand of optimism could not be sustained, however, as stock prices fell and the country plunged into economic turmoil.

I n this present era of applied invention, of trained intelligence, of old industries expanded, checked or displaced, of whole new industries rising with the magician's wand of Invention, of high speed in the creation of wealth and possessions, we have a fluid economic structure that challenges the imagination. The social habits, indeed the individual character of our people, are under the influence of new and vast forces. The scene shifts almost hourly. The world of everyday has become a fairyland.

In new industry, the ten-year-old radio developed under the proper stimulant of profits, nevertheless records the day's magic of radio programs projected into the hitherto menacing silences of the Polar South and instantly acknowledged by those intrepid explorers whose deadly isolation is thus relieved.

In industry claimed as both old and new, we have the continuing marvel of the automobile. The one million cars owned in America with the birth of this Chamber [the United States Chamber of Commerce, founded in 1912], have grown to twenty-five million. It is the chief reliance of steel and plate glass and leather and rubber. A rival itself of railroad transportation, it nevertheless provides the equivalent of four weeks' exclusive employment in every year of all the railroad facilities of this country for itself and its associates alone.

## Improved Industrial Techniques

In industry we have the almost daily commonplace of billion dollar corporations, the climax of merged units, and owned by hundreds of thousands of individual stock holders. We have as well the myriad modest beginnings of new industry under individual ambition, hoping also to become in time the basis of far-flung industry.

> In banking, there has evolved the unit of two billions of resources under a single direction, assuring unlimited credit for vast enterprise.

In production we have mass methods, supplying a range of goods to the Five-and-Ten Cent store beyond the imagination of yesterday, yet paralleled by the quality market of individual appeal which absorbs the $300 basket of flowers and the $500 bottle of perfume.

In advertising, we have the magazine of its million readers, in which the price of a single page for a single number would build a comfortable family home.

In mining, technique and daring now extract large profits from vast daily tonnage of such infinitesimal metal content as was disregarded by mining science of a recent past. One western mine alone moves annually more earth than was excavated in the entire Panama Canal.

In construction, a single city in a single week issued building permits for four structures that tower fifty to sixty stories—temples of business dwarfing the Eiffel Tower.

In agriculture, farm adaptability to modern machine invention has disbanded the old seasonal migratory army of farm serfs and is rebuilding farm prosperity, ranging from the low cost machine production of the Great Plains to the redeemed abandoned farms of the East, now recreated into farm homes resting securely on daily motor marketing of quality production.

In banking, there has evolved the unit of two billions of resources under a single direction, assuring unlimited credit for vast enterprise, yet human enough to systematize a myriad small emergency loans on individual character.

## Advances in Transportation and Communication

In transportation, we have doubled in a decade the tonnage of railroad freight, and then have paralleled our railways with a new army of truck drivers that now almost equals the total of railway employees. We have, besides, enrolled an army of six hundred thousand chauffeurs, and made the open road not only the servant of industry but also the door to health and pleasure.

In passenger travel, we have restored to the open road the romance of changing view, the hospitality of wayside inns, and our cities welcome their visitors through the sightly boulevard, not the untidy back alley.

In airways, we have cut the four-month transcontinental voyage of the covered wagon to the twenty-six-hour air service, coast to coast, and made every inland city a possible world port.

> One is most impressed by the truth that industry, operating primarily for profit, must nevertheless intertwine itself with social service.

In communication, we have, during the life of this Chamber, increased our telephones from seven million to nineteen million, and by the miracle of ocean radio have brought to every single instrument the access to twenty-eight million receivers, out of the world's thirty-three million.

In public discussion, we have built the audience of sixty million radio hearers for a single voice, and public questions are today presented to our citizens with the intimacy of the fireside discussion.

In amusement, the motion-picture temples seat a daily audience of fourteen million, and with their picture fiction give also, through eye and ear, the current news of a now contracting world.

In education, we have lifted the country child from muddy road trudging to swift motor delivery at consolidated schools, for a grade of instruction impossible in the little red schoolhouse. Great universities, supported by a sense of stewardship of great wealth, enroll today an army of trained intelligence double that of all the world besides.

## Ties Between Industry and Social Service

When one attempts to measure the full effects of this vast ferment illustrated by these highlights of modern industry, one is most impressed by the truth that industry, operating primarily for profit, must nevertheless intertwine itself with social service.

For example, the modern refrigerator, perfected glass and metal containers for the year-wide preservation of seasonal foods; the automatic oil heater with its equably preserved temperatures in the home; the vacuum cleaner with its daily cleanliness; all these and a thousand other household appliances are designed, produced and marketed under the stimulus of healthful business profit. But the social service that follows incidentally but surely is shown in the falling tables of illness and the constant improvement in the actuarial death tables. Behind these figures rests a whole human story of relieved anxiety, distress and sorrow. . . .

> More millions of our people have found that investments in sound and well managed American industries . . . have oftentimes made their daydreams of fortunate investment come actually true.

## Industrial Success Leads to National Wealth

Applied invention today, quick in discovery through the research laboratory and readily adapted into industry itself, has so quickened the creation of national wealth that the annual national income of our people has risen during the life of this Chamber from thirty-two billion dollars to ninety billion, annually. In the distribution of that wealth under our free society, the savings of our people have risen during that period from eight billion dollars to twenty-eight billion dollars. In the distribution of the ownership of this expanding industry the life of this Chamber has witnessed such striking examples in many directions, as is instanced by the increase of stockholders in the American Telephone and Telegraph Company [the telecommunications company now known as AT&T] from fifty-three thousand to four hundred fifty thousand. In the training of our people for the safe and profitable reinvestment of their current earnings, the new capital issues absorbed annually by investors has during the life of this Chamber increased twenty times.

In this rapid creation of aggregate wealth and in the inevitable inequalities and confusion which must accompany the distribution of that wealth even under the free play of the fairest influences, we must expect many puzzling problems. As individual savings have increased there has been an increased understanding of the possibilities of profitable investment. As long as men live, they will dream dreams and build castles in the air. If in the past the investment of too many people too often trended toward the wild-cat oil well and the distant gold mine, it can at least be humanly understood as a groping for some part of ownership in the swift miracle of America's developing prosperity. Then in recent years, more millions of our people have found that investments in sound and well managed American industries in this great expanding market have oftentimes made their day-dreams of fortunate investment come actually true. The expanding role of individual stockholders in great American industry shows this tendency to be true. It emphasizes the sober responsibility resting upon the management and direction of great industries whose ownership is spread through many thousands of small investors.

If, in the security market, excesses have developed in the installment plan of purchase of ownership securities in American industries, it again brings to the front the responsibility of those sections of American business which should tender sober and experienced advice, yet preserving the creative value of the ambition to better the individual fortune. . . .

## American Potential Is Infinite

By favor of Nature and by a freedom from the handicap of age-old custom or habit, and by the energy of its people stimulated by a political philosophy of equal opportunity, America has found the key to universal individual welfare. America has learned that national wealth is the aggregate of individual possession and attainment and that the stimulated production of the individual inevitably builds higher the aggregate of national possession.

It is no accident that the relative national wealth, for example, of the United States, as against Great Britain, is almost the exact relationship of the relative per capita horsepower—four and one-half to one. It is no accident that the United States also stands at the head in equipping each worker with power and machines that enlarge his daily production, making more things to divide among the individual homes of America.

The proof of the effect on national and individual prosperity and its industrial truth is indicated by the gamut of machinery equipment per capita, running from twenty-four dollars in the United States down to one dollar per capita for Russia.

New York's Chrysler Building was erected in 1930 as a testament to the success of the auto industry. (Andrew Harrer/ Bloomberg via Getty Images.)

There are vast populations to learn these truths, and to learn that the needs and aspirations of mankind are limitless, and that the opportunity to work and earn is the beginning of a rising opportunity for possession and use. The field that calls to American youth and American capital throughout the world is limitless.

# Black Tuesday: The Stock Market Crash of 1929

### *The New York Times*

In the following viewpoint, the *New York Times* reports on the events of October 29, 1929—Black Tuesday, the culmination of several days of declining stock values as large and small investors dumped billions of dollars of stock on the New York markets. The *Times* claims that the collapse started in September 1929 when a few major business empires folded both in the United States and abroad. The newspaper reports that the selling off of shares in the United States continued, however, despite industry's best attempts to stabilize the market. The *Times* concludes that it was not overextended small-time investors who caused the crash but rich men who panicked at the first sign of declining prices. Still, the newspaper notes that bankers and industrialists remained optimistic that the downturn would be short-lived.

---

SOURCE. "Stocks Collapse in 16,410,030—Share Day, but Rally at Close Cheers Brokers; Bankers Optimistic, to Continue Aid," *New York Times*, October 30, 1929. Copyright © 1929 by The New York Times Company. Reproduced by permission.

Stock prices virtually collapsed yesterday [October 29, 1929], swept downward with gigantic losses in the most disastrous trading day in the stock market's history. Billions of dollars in open market values were wiped out as prices crumbled under the pressure of liquidation of securities which had to be sold at any price.

There was an impressive rally just at the close, which brought many leading stocks back from 4 to 14 points from their lowest points of the day.

Trading on the New York Stock Exchange aggregated 16,410,030 shares; on the Curb [now the AMEX stock exchange], 7,096,300 shares were dealt in [put up for sale]. Both totals far exceeded any previous day's dealings.

From every point of view, in the extent of losses sustained, in total turnover, in the number of speculators wiped out, the day was the most disastrous in Wall Street's history. Hysteria swept the country and stocks went overboard for just what they would bring at forced sale.

Efforts to estimate yesterday's market losses in dollars are futile because of the vast number of securities quoted over the counter and on out-of-town exchanges on which no calculations are possible. However, it was estimated that 880 issues, on the New York Stock Exchange, lost between $8,000,000,000 and $9,000,000,000 yesterday. Added to that loss is to be reckoned the depreciation on issues on the Curb Market, in the over the counter market and on other exchanges.

## Signs of Optimism

There were two cheerful notes, however, which sounded through the pall of gloom which overhung the financial centres of the country. One was the brisk rally of stocks at the close, on tremendous buying by those who believe that prices have sunk too low. The other was that the liquidation has been so violent, as well as widespread, that many bankers, brokers and industrial leaders expressed the belief last night that it now has run its course.

A further note of optimism in the soundness of fundamentals was sounded by the directors of the United States Steel Corporation and the American Can Company, each of which declared an extra dividend of $1 a share at their late afternoon meetings.

Banking support, which would have been impressive and successful under ordinary circumstances, was swept violently aside, as block after block of stock, tremendous in proportions, deluged the market. Bid prices placed by bankers, industrial leaders and brokers trying to halt the decline were crashed through violently, their orders were filled, and quotations plunged downward in a day of disorganization, confusion and financial impotence.

## An End to the Downturn Is Expected

That there will be a change today seemed likely from statements made last night by financial and business leaders. Organized support will be accorded to the market from the start, it is believed, but those who are staking their all on the country's leading securities are placing a great deal of confidence, too, in the expectation that there will be an overnight change in sentiment; that the counsel of cool heads will prevail and that the mob psychology which has been so largely responsible for the market's debacle will be broken.

The fact that the leading stocks were able to rally in the final fifteen minutes of trading yesterday was considered a good omen, especially as the weakest period of the day had developed just prior to that time and the minimum prices for the day had then been established. It was a quick run-up which followed

> "The market on the rampage is no respecter of persons. It washed fortune after fortune away yesterday and financially crippled thousands of individuals in all parts of the world."

The plummeting stock market drew crowds to Wall Street in the days before Black Tuesday on October 29, 1929. (Popperfoto/Getty Images.)

the announcement that the American Can directors had declared an extra dividend of $1. The advances in leading stocks in this last fifteen minutes represented a measurable snapback from the lows. American Can gained 10; United States Steel common, 7½, General Electric, 12; New York Central, 14½, Anaconda Copper, 9½; Chrysler Motors 5¼; Montgomery Ward, 4¼ and Johns Manville, 8. Even with these recoveries, the losses of these particular stocks, and practically all others, were staggering.

Yesterday's market crash was one which largely affected rich men, institutions, investment trusts and others who participate in the stock market on a broad and intelligent scale. It was not the margin traders who were caught in the rush to sell, but the rich men of the country who are able to swing blocks of 5,000,

10,000 up to 100,000 shares of high-priced stocks. They went overboard with no more consideration than the little trader who was swept out on the first day of the market's upheaval, whose prices, even at their lowest of last Thursday [October 24, 1929], now look high in comparison.

The market on the rampage is no respecter of persons. It washed fortune after fortune away yesterday [October 29] and financially crippled thousands of individuals in all parts of the world. It was not until after the market had closed that the financial district began to realize that a good-sized rally had taken place and that there was a stopping place on the downgrade for good stocks.

## Third Day of Collapse

The market has now passed through three days of collapse, and so violent has it been that most authorities believe that the end is not far away. It started last Thursday, when 12,800,000 shares were dealt in on the Exchange, and holders of stocks commenced to learn just what a decline in the market means. This was followed by a moderate rally on Friday and entirely normal conditions on Saturday, with fluctuations on a comparatively narrow scale and with the efforts of the leading bankers to stabilize the market evidently successful. But the storm broke anew on Monday, with prices slaughtered in every direction, to be followed by yesterday's tremendous trading of 16,410,030 shares.

Sentiment had been generally unsettled since the first of September. Market prices had then reached peak levels, and, try as they would, pool operators and other friends of the market could not get them higher. It was a gradual downward sag, gaining momentum as it went on, then to break out into an open market smash in which the good, the bad, and indifferent stocks went down alike. Thousands of traders were able to weather the first storm and answered their margin calls;[1] thousands fell by

> In that first thirty minutes of trading, stocks were poured out in 5,000, 10,000, 20,000 and 50,000 share blocks at tremendous sacrifices.

the wayside Monday and again yesterday, unable to meet the demands of their brokers that their accounts be protected [i.e., adequately funded].

There was no quibbling at all between customer and broker yesterday. In any case where margin became thin a peremptory call went out. If there was no immediate answer the stock was sold out "at the market" for just what it would bring. Thousands, sold out on the decline and amid the confusion, found themselves in debt to their brokers last night.

## Wall Street Is Weathering the Storm

Three factors stood out most prominently last night after the market's close. They were:

- Wall Street has been able to weather the storm with but a single Curb failure, small in size, and no member of the New York Stock Exchange has announced himself unable to meet commitments.

- The smashing decline has brought stocks down to a level where, in the opinion of leading bankers and industrialists, they are a buy on their merits and prospects, and brokers have so advised their customers.

- The very violence of the liquidation, which has cleaned up many hundreds of sore spots which honeycombed the market, and the expected ability of the market to right itself, since millions of shares of stock have passed to strong hands from weak ones.

One of the factors which Wall Street failed to take into consideration throughout the entire debacle was that the banking consortium has no idea of putting stocks up or to save any individuals from loss, but that its sole purpose was to alleviate the wave of financial hysteria sweeping the country and provide bids, at some price, where needed. It was pointed out in many quarters that no broad liquidating movement in the stock market has ever been stopped by so-called good buying. This is helpful, of course, but it never stops an avalanche of liquidation, as was this one.

There is only one factor, it was pointed out, which can and always does stop a down swing—that is, the actual cessation of forced liquidation. It is usually the case, too, that when the last of the forced selling has been completed the stock market always faces a wide-open gap in which there are practically no offerings of securities at all. When that point is reached, buying springs up from everywhere and always accounts for a sharp, almost perpendicular recovery in the best stocks. The opinion was widely expressed in Wall Street last night that that point has been reached, or at least very nearly reached.

> "Men and women crowded the brokerage offices, even those who have been long since wiped out, and followed the figures on the tape. . . . It was the consensus of bankers and brokers alike that no such scenes ever again will be witnessed by this generation."

## Huge Blocks Offered at Opening

The opening bell on the Stock Exchange released such a flood of selling as has never before been witnessed in this country. The failure of the market to rally consistently on the previous day, the tremendous shrinkage of open market values and the wave of hysteria which appeared to sweep the country brought an avalanche of stock to the market to be sold at whatever price it would bring.

From the very first quotation until thirty minutes after 10 o'clock it was evident that the day's market would be an unprecedented one. In that first thirty minutes of trading, stocks were poured out in 5,000, 10,000, 20,000 and 50,000 share blocks at tremendous sacrifices as compared with the previous closing. The declines ranged from a point or so to as much as 29½ points, and the reports of opening prices brought selling into the market in confused volume that has never before been equaled.

In this first half hour of trading on the Stock Exchange a total of 3,250,800 shares were dealt in. The volume of the first twenty-six blocks of stock dealt in at the opening totaled more than 630,000 shares.

There was simply no near-by demand for even the country's leading industrial and railroad shares, and many millions of dollars in values were lost in the first quotations tapped out. All considerations other than to get rid of the stock at any price were brushed aside.

## Crowds Gather at Brokerages

Wall Street was a street of vanished hopes, of curiously silent apprehension and of a sort of paralyzed hypnosis yesterday. Men and women crowded the brokerage offices, even those who have been long since wiped out, and followed the figures on the tape. Little groups gathered here and there to discuss the fall in prices in hushed and awed tones. They were participating in the making of financial history. It was the consensus of bankers and brokers alike that no such scenes ever again will be witnessed by this generation. To most of those who have been in the market it is all the more awe-inspiring because their financial history is limited to bull markets [markets characterized by rising prices].

The machinery of the New York Stock Exchange and the Curb market were unable to handle the tremendous volume of trading which went over them. Early in the day they kept up well, because most of the trading was in big blocks, but as the day progressed the tickers fell further and further behind, and as on the previous big days of this week and last it was only by printing late quotations of stocks on the bond tickers and by the 10-minute flashes on stock prices put out by Dow, Jones & Co. and the Wall Street News Bureau that the financial district could get any idea of what was happening in the wild mob of brokers on the Exchange and the Curb.

## Early Signs of Decline

The bull market, the most extensive in the history of the country, started in the [Calvin] Coolidge Administration [1923–1929] and reached its height with a tremendous burst of speculation in the public utility issues, the flames of speculation being fed by mergers, new groupings, combinations and good earnings.

The highest prices were reached in early September [1929]. At that time the market had a quick break and an equally rapid recovery. Then started a slow sag. Two developments, not considered important at the time, served to start the ball rolling downhill. The first of these was the refusal of the Massachusetts Public Service Commission to permit the Boston Edison Company to split its shares; the second was the collapse of a pool in International Combustion Engineering shares on the Stock Exchange, an over-exploited industrial which had been pushed across 100 by a pool and which crashed when the corporation passed its dividend.

In the meanwhile, the Hatry failure[2] abroad had diverted a tremendous volume of selling to the United States, and under these influences the market continued to sag until it literally crumpled of its own weight.

### Notes

1. To answer a margin call is to deposit money into an institution to back up stocks that have been purchased with money borrowed from the institution.
2. The Hatry failure was the collapse of Clarence Hatry's business empire in the U.K. due to fraud and forged stock certificates.

# The Hardship of Farmers During the Depression

## Donald R. Murphy

In the viewpoint that follows, U.S. journalist Donald R. Murphy, writing in 1932, describes the response of Midwestern farmers to more than a decade of falling prices for agricultural goods. Following World War I, as Europe reestablished its agricultural production, U.S. farmers no longer had a market for selling the surplus of goods they had grown accustomed to producing during the war. As a result, the prices of these goods began to decline. Murphy explains the hardship the farmers faced as the price drops grew steeper during the onset of the Great Depression. He also details the Farmers' Holidays—grassroots strikes organized around the country in an attempt to limit the amount of goods on the market and thus increase the price of goods to a level that covered the cost of production and provided a living wage for the farmers. Donald R. Murphy was a journalist for Midwestern farm papers that catered to the rural reader during the Great Depression. Murphy was also a

**SOURCE.** Donald R. Murphy, "The Farmers Go on Strike," *Americans View Their Dust Bowl Experience.* Edited by John R. Wunder, Frances W. Kaye, and Vernon Carstensen. University Press of Colorado, 1999.

longtime friend and supporter of New Deal–era secretary of agriculture Henry A. Wallace.

On a paved road in northwestern Iowa, a truck loaded with cream cans bowls along. Suddenly a long-chain stretched between two trees bars the road.

From the sides of the highway, where they have been lounging under the trees in the tall grass, a dozen tanned men, the leader waving a red flag, bar the road. There are pitchforks handy for puncturing tires, rocks for cracking windshields, clubs to persuade the truck driver.

"Where you bound?"

"Sioux City."

"What you got?"

"Cream."

"Turn around and get outa here. Don't you know the Farmers' Holiday is on?"

Usually the truck backs up. Sometimes the driver takes a chance and tries to break through. A few of these chance-takers have finally retreated with broken windshields and punctured tires. The cream has been dumped in the road.

This is a picture of the most dramatic phase of the Farmers' Holiday—the attempt of a group of Middle Western farmers to enforce a strike designed to stop the movement of all farm products to market.

## Twelve Years of Depression for Farmers

In a dozen counties in northwestern Iowa, and to a lesser degree in other counties, farmers are picketing the roads and stopping shipments. In several small towns produce buyers have agreed to shut up shop during the holiday. Elevators are considering refusing to buy grain until the holiday is over. Up in the Sioux City area special deputies have been sworn in and are riding a few trucks daily through the picket line.

In some cases truck drivers and farmers refuse to accept protection by deputies and stay home. "I've got to stay on living here," said one. "I guess I'll leave the truck in the shed for a while." Leaders of the strike, disclaiming any desire to use violence, insist that social ostracism of strike breakers will hold farmers in line. A farmer with hostile neighbors is helpless at threshing and at silo-filling time.

> For [farmers] the depression has lasted, not three years, but twelve.

The strike is the culmination of a growing sense of injustice by corn-belt farmers. Specifically it is the response to years of exhortation by Milo Reno, veteran leader of the Iowa Farmers' Union, and his associates. For years, Reno has told farmers that eventually they would have to go on strike and starve city people into giving the farmer a square deal. The farmers that are supporting the holiday have backed the old McNary-Haugen bill[1], the more recent Frazier bill to refinance farm mortgages at a low rate of interest, and other farm legislation of a so-called "radical" type. They have seen these bills beaten and have watched farm prices go down and down since the big crash in 1920. For them the depression has lasted, not three years, but twelve.

## The Farmers' Strike Begins

This year [1932] farms are being taking over by mortgage holders at an increasing rate. Renters are finding that this year's crop will not pay cash rent. Farm buying power is down to 50 percent of the pre-war average.

To many farmers, it seemed that the time for direct action had come. Early this spring the Iowa Farmers' Union, traditional leader of left-wing movements in farm affairs, began to discuss plans for Farmers' Holiday

during which all farmers would be pledged to refuse to sell any farm products. The agitation was continued, mainly in Iowa but also in several other Midwestern states, through the summer. Organizers carried pledge cards for farmers to sign. Finally the Iowa strike was called to start August 8 [1932].

In a manifesto adopted by farmers from Iowa, North and South Dakota, Illinois, Minnesota, and Nebraska, at a meeting in Des Moines, August 15, the organizers of the movement said:

> Self-preservation is still the first law of nature and we
> agree to keep all of our products which can possibly be

High winds compounded with drought and poor farming methods turned the Great Plains into the Dust Bowl in the 1930s. (Buyenlarge/ Getty Images.)

kept on the farms and hold same until the time shall have arrived when farm products shall bring a market price equal to the cost of production.

We pledge ourselves to protect one another in the actual possession of our necessary homes, livestock and machinery as against all claimants.

## Farmers Seek Cost of Production for Goods

What is "cost of production"? The Farmers' Union works it out this way: Allow the farmer 5 percent on his investment in real estate, 7 percent on investments in personal property and equipment, and $100 a month for his own labor. To obtain this return, the union figures that on an average 160-acre Iowa farm with normal production, prices would have to be as follows: ninety-two cents a bushel for corn, forty-nine cents a bushel for oats, $11.25 for hogs, thirty-five cents a dozen for eggs, and sixty-two cents a pound for butter fat. On Monday, August 8, when the Farmers' Holiday was supposed to start, the farm prices on these products were: twenty-two cents for corn, eleven cents for oats, $3.85 for hogs, fifteen cents for eggs, and eighteen cents for butter fat.

The call for the holiday directed farmers to stay off the market for thirty days or until prices reached "cost of production." Iowa was to start the ball rolling. Minnesota, Illinois, and South Dakota were expected to come in the second or third week. North Dakota and Nebraska were also listed as prospects.

The first week of the strike in Iowa showed few results. Receipts of farm products at the different markets dropped off little if at all. In the second week, however, a new factor entered. The milk producers at Sioux City, who are getting only two cents a quart for whole milk, went on strike. These farmers began to hold up milk trucks and dump the milk.

The area around Sioux City has a good many Farmers' Union members and many more supporters of the Farmers' Holiday. These farmers seized the opportunity opened by the milk strike, joined the milk-strike pickets and began to stop, not only milk trucks, but trucks carrying any farm produce to town. The movement spread to an area including many of the counties in northwestern Iowa. Picketing, sometimes accompanied by mass action to turn back trucks, was common on many main highways. Even in northwestern Iowa, however, many towns were unaffected by the movement.

> Even conservative farmers who take no part in the Farmers' Holiday movement seem pleased to see the bankers squirm when their own trick is turned against them.

## Revenge for the Bank Holidays

It is not entirely an accident that the area in which the Farmers' Holiday is strongest is roughly the same area of recent Bank Holidays [periods when banks closed for a set number of days to halt high numbers of withdrawals]. In this section lately, banks have adopted an extra-legal device to protect themselves against frightened depositors. They have persuaded the mayor in each town to declare a holiday, with all business houses closed, for a week or ten-day period. During this time, crews of business men have made the rounds of the depositors and obtained statements from them permitting the bank to retain the deposits for a period of some months, with the depositor not being allowed to check out any of his money except in specified small amounts.

The campaign to get these statements from depositors has been handled like the old Liberty Loan drives. Farmers reluctant to give up their deposits because they have been accumulated to meet interest or taxes, have been harassed by teams of solicitors until they signed. In cases where farmers have refused to sign, and banks have reopened, the banks have refused to let the non-signers have their money. The Bank Holiday has furnished a fine argument for the backers of the Farmers' Holiday. They have used it vigorously. Even conservative farmers who take no part in the Farmers' Holiday movement seem pleased to see the bankers squirm when their own trick is turned against them.

## Cooperation Between Farmers

Right now, in the third week of the Iowa strike, the usual guess is that the holiday will be confined to northwestern Iowa. The amount of produce going to market in that section is being cut down, but not enough to affect prices. If the balance of the state and other states join in, some real reduction in the flow of produce to market might be obtained. Of course, even if this should happen, the resultant rise in the price of farm products would hardly help the holiday supporter. The better prices would go to the farmers who continue to sell their products. As soon as the holiday backers would throw their products on the market again, any scarcity-induced rise in prices would collapse and the holiday backers would get the resulting low prices. The backers of the holiday claim that once higher prices are obtained they will be maintained by a system of feeding farm products into the market gradually.

> It relieves a farmer's feelings a good deal to throw a rock through a windshield or to take any positive step . . . that seems to lead toward better prices.

In the long run the pledge of these farmers to protect each other against foreclosure may turn out to be more important than the strike. Certainly, even if the holiday ends with no real results, the irritation of farm people against low prices will not cease. There will be another outbreak. It may logically take the form of neighborhood defense against foreclosures. Such a program would have considerably more backing than the present strike. Even now, conservative farmers who see no success in the holiday movement express considerable sympathy for the project or for any project aimed at raising farm prices and keeping farmers on their own farms.

## Farmers Feel Better After Taking Action

Farmers have submitted with surprising meekness to a long period of deflation. Orthodox and conservative, they have followed the conventional methods of trying to obtain reform by petitioning Congress for action. Instead of getting help, they have seen [President Calvin] Coolidge veto two McNary-Haugen bills, and have seen [President Herbert] Hoover block farm bills at the last session. Meanwhile farm prices have slipped lower and lower; farmer after farmer has met foreclosure, and no serious attempt—or so it seems to farmers—has been made by those in power to improve conditions. After twelve years of this it relieves a farmer's feelings a good deal to throw a rock through a windshield or to take any positive step, no matter how futile it may ultimately prove to be, that seems to lead toward better prices.

The Farmers' Holiday will probably fail in obtaining any substantial reduction of the flow of farm products to market; it will undoubtedly fail in an attempt to affect prices to any extent. It remains, however, a significant symptom of the state of mind of a great conservative class which has borne depression for twelve years and which is finally ready to employ radical measures that seem to give it a chance to save itself from general bankruptcy. Unless farm prices go up this will not be the last outbreak in the corn belt.

## Note

1. The McNary-Haugen bill was written to create sustainable prices for agriculture goods through government purchase of surpluses.

# The Dust Bowl Shows Promise for Regeneration

## Ben Hibbs

Ben Hibbs, a former reporter for the *Saturday Evening Post*, reviews in the following viewpoint the formation of the Dust Bowl, a portion of the central United States farm belt in which poor farming practices and drought resulted in soil erosion and dust storms that nearly shut down agricultural production for several years in the early 1930s. Hibbs asserts that the blowing sandstorms and lack of water drove many farmers out of the region, forcing them to abandon their farms and their livelihood. He recounts, however, that those who stayed eventually availed themselves of government aid in the form of the Soil Conservation Service. This organization, formed in 1935, helped farmers develop techniques to retain rainfall, employ crop rotation, and plant cover crops to keep topsoil from blowing away. Hibbs contends that these strategies were already show-

**SOURCE.** Ben Hibbs, "The Dust Bowl Can Be Saved," *Saturday Evening Post*, vol. 210, December 18, 1937, pp. 16–17 and 77–82. Copyright © 1937 Saturday Evening Post Society. Reproduced by permission.

ing promising results in the first two years of implementation and that the Dust Bowl was steadily being shrunk because of the concerted efforts of the government and the farmers.

Due north of Dalhart, Texas, fifty miles away, across an empty landscape, is Boise City, in the Oklahoma Panhandle. There was a time when the James Brothers' ranch occupied nearly all of the intervening prairies. It was one of the vast cattle outfits of the southern high plains—a domain of 600,000 acres, owned and leased. Short, succulent grama grasses clothed the land, with here and there a patch of big bluestem, which often grew as high as a man's armpits.

Not long ago I sat in a hotel at Dalhart, talking with Andy James. The great ranch was broken up and sold piecemeal when wheat invaded the Panhandle. The prairies over which the James herds once roamed now lie in the heart of the dust bowl. I asked Andy James if he regretted the coming of the tractor and the plow.

"No." The old cowman's answer was emphatic. "This is good farming country, if it is farmed right. We have raised some fine crops on these high plains, and we can do it again. But," he qualified again, "we've got to change our methods."

Andy James grinned wryly. "I may as well make my confession now as later. You see, I helped create the dust bowl. When the farmers began to come in and the price of land rose, we relinquished our grass leases and gradually sold off the range on which we hold title. But we did keep about 26,000 acres. Today I've got 20,000 acres in grass and about 6,000 acres under cultivation. I'm a cattleman still, but I'm also a farmer."

## The Farmers Are to Blame

"Now let's get this straight. I don't regret the breaking out of that 6,000 acres. Most of it is good farm land. Some of our self-appointed experts, you know, have gone around the country saying that we should never have plowed up an acre of the Panhandle. I don't agree with them. There are fields which, because of the soil characteristics, should have been left in grass. In the main, however, our blunder was not in breaking the sod but in the farming methods we used afterwards.

> Range lands appeared to be as dead as the moon, and the pastures in the proximity of plowed fields were rapidly being silted over.

"We must have thought we were farming back on the heavy lands of Iowa or Illinois. Or, more likely, we just didn't think. Anyway, we didn't give much attention to the conserving of moisture and humus, and we went right on betting on wheat in the dry years when we should have been getting our fields under cover crops. Naturally, in a country of low rainfall and light soils, it didn't take long to get the land in a prime condition to blow. Then the big drought hit us [in 1930] and we were in a nice mess.

"But it isn't too late to save the dust bowl for farming. The scientific men are developing methods that will do the job, and I hope that most of us are going to be intelligent enough to follow their lead. Suppose," the rancher proposed, "we get in the car and go take a look."

And so that afternoon I saw a considerable portion of Dallam County. During the ensuing week, I traveled the length and breadth of the dust bowl—the five-state area embracing the Texas and Oklahoma Panhandles, Southwestern Kansas, Southeastern Colorado and Northeastern New Mexico. Two years ago, in the autumn of 1935, I journeyed over this same region. What has happened in the meantime is significant.

## Improving Conditions in the Panhandle

In 1935, the plight of the entire dust bowl was about as bad as possible. The soil of an area more than twice as large as all New England was on the loose. Even on days of low wind velocity, banners of gray dust played across the barren fields. Much of the crop land was so badly drifted and hummocked that some soils experts doubted that it would ever produce again. Range lands appeared to be as dead as the moon, and the pastures in the proximity of plowed fields were rapidly being silted over. The Soil Conservation Service, a nonpolitical arm of the Department of Agriculture, had just begun work and there was a note of grimness and uncertainty in the talk of its staff.

Today the dust bowl still exists, but it has shrunk. Conditions in some counties are as bad as they were in 1935; in other localities there has been great improvement. Unless rainfall is abnormally good during the next six months, the black blizzards will continue through another crop year. Yet there are many encouraging signs.

In the southern half of the Texas Panhandle the worst of the crisis seems to be past, temporarily at least. Rainfall there was better this year, and more strategically timed for the maturing of crops. North of Amarillo to the Canadian River, precipitation was spotty, but in some localities sufficient to produce a harvest. As a result, the wheat counties of the Texas Panhandle checked in this year with a crop estimated at 20,000,000 bushels. An average harvest is about 32,000,000. In the southern end of the dust bowl, the cotton crop was not yet in the bale when I was there, but advance estimates were highly optimistic. . . .

> In the autumn of 1935 I often drove as much as forty miles across those vacant plains [of the Dust Bowl] without seeing a blade of anything green.

In the three huge counties of the Oklahoma Panhandle this year's [wheat] harvest was 450,000 bushels; in 1929 the take was 13,593,821 bushels.

## Signs of Regeneration

Counties have lost as much as 60 per cent of their rural population. A year ago [1936], the Resettlement Administration—now the FSA—made a check in seven counties of Southeastern Colorado, found 2,878 farmhouses occupied and 2,811 empty. In addition, there were 1,522 abandoned home sites where only the wind-swept ruins remained—a tragic reminder of other droughts. By the end of the 1936 crop year approximately 52 per cent of the land in these same seven counties had been abandoned—for the time being, at least.

The exodus from the northern portions of the dust bowl continued through the summer of 1937, but not at the pace of 1935 and 1936. Those who remain usually are better equipped to stick it out and wait for the rains.

> The Soil Conservation Service has done a rather amazing job of demonstrating that fertility still abides in most of the dust-bowl lands.

That is the bleak side—the beating the people have taken, and are still taking in many localities. There is a happier side.

In the autumn of 1935 I often drove as much as forty miles across those vacant plains without seeing a blade of anything green. This year I followed many of the same roads. Green fields of milo, Sudan, broom corn and other drought-resistant row crops dotted nearly every portion of the dust bowl. Many farmers, finally having given up wheat until it rains, are turning to the spring-planted crops which often pan out when wheat will not. It is probably the best thing that could happen to the blow lands, because after maize is harvested in the fall, the heavy, tough stubble remains on the ground through the winter and early spring. The soil in those fields is lashed down for the coming season.

Moreover, Nature, like a wounded animal, seems to have a habit of nursing her own injuries. Large areas of abandoned land, which, two years ago, took to the air every time the wind rose, now support a rank growth of weeds, Russian thistles and sage. That isn't recovery in the long-time sense of the word, but weeds do put a stop to wind erosion.

The net result of the turn from wheat to maize, and of Nature's own weed crop, is that more fields are now stabilized than at any time since the black blizzards first began to make the headlines. And every field that is put under cover gives a better chance to control adjacent lands.

## The Soil Conservation Service Steps In

The most encouraging fact which has been demonstrated is that the fertility of the dust bowl has not been destroyed. Not yet! In 1935 there was much controversy as to whether a considerable portion of the blown and hummocked farm lands would ever grow another crop. Even the Soil Conservation Service—which in its early months in that area was too vocal on matters which had been insufficiently investigated—made a hasty survey and announced that 4,016,562 acres had been "destroyed" by wind erosion.

At that time I laid this figure before Ray I. Throckmorton, chief agronomist at Kansas State Agricultural College, who has spent twenty-six years studying the farming of the high plains. Throckmorton is probably more intimately acquainted with soils, crops and farmers in the northern half of the dust bowl than any other man. His opinion of the land-destruction figure was expressed in a word, "Absurd!" Dust-bowl farmers also made a one-word comment. They said, "Nuts!"

During the ensuing two years the Soil Conservation Service has done a rather amazing job of demonstrating that fertility still abides in most of the dust-bowl lands. And no one is happier than the conservationists themselves to see their lugubrious estimates of 1935 discredited. "Of course we made mistakes," they say

The Soil Conservation Service implemented various techniques to remedy Dust Bowl conditions. (David E. Sherman/Time & Life Pictures/Getty Images.)

now. "Large-scale wind erosion was a new agricultural problem." . . .

## Contour Farming Saves Water

The program of improved farming which is being urged for the dust bowl is predicated upon three basic points: (1) conservation of moisture, (2) the consisted use of cover crops, and (3) a cessation of the disastrous practice of planting wheat in a dry seedbed.

Contour farming is not new. A century and a half ago, Thomas Jefferson urged his fellow farmers to plow their furrows around the slopes instead of up and down hill. In many of the older billy regions, farmers have long laid their plantings around the gradient of the land.

They have to or their soil would be washed away. On the level plains of the West, however, the grower has usually followed the lines of the compass. But at the Goodwell experiment station, in the Oklahoma Panhandle, was an agronomist who had an idea. His name was H.H. Finnell.

Finnell had noticed that on lands which appeared to be as level as a floor, but often had a gradient of 1 per cent or more, much of the rainfall was lost. Normal precipitation in that country ranged from sixteen to twenty inches yearly, but it often came in bursts—sometimes as much as three inches in an hour. Water coursed off the fields into dry lake beds and ditches.

> Terracing costs about $1.75 an acre, and a properly farmed terrace lasts forever.

Why not, Finnell asked himself, have an engineer run guide lines through the fields—each line on a level, across the slope of the land—and farm accordingly? The furrows made by tillage implements would swing back and forth in broad curves, but what of it? Instead of running off, water would cascade into the furrows, back up there and sink into the soil. He tried it and began to get surprisingly large yields from land thus handled.

Later he went a step further and threw up broad, low terraces across the fields—also on the contour. The terraces—about forty feet broad at the base, from eight to fifteen inches high, and placed from 150 to 300 feet apart—seemed to catch additional water which escaped the furrows, and also furnished permanent guide lines for contour farming. They were so broad and low, their slopes so gradual, that crops were grown upon them.

Finnell had been at his experiments some years when the great drought struck. He was able to convince Dr. Hugh H. Bennett, director of the Soil Conservation Service, that his methods were effective. Finnell, named to head work of the Service in the dust bowl, blocked out thirteen large demonstrational projects. He built up a technical staff of men who, as far as possible, were familiar with the region.

The typical demonstrational project is of 25,000 acres. The lands are privately owned. Farmers come into the projects voluntarily, sit around the table with the Soil Conservation men and plan their operations. They must then abide by the scheme laid out. They continue to do their own farming, but the Government performs certain tasks, such as the building of terraces. Terracing costs about $1.75 an acre, and a properly farmed terrace lasts forever.

Another practice urged by the conservationists is strip-cropping—the planting of cover crops, such as the sorghums and Sudan grass, in alternate strips with wheat. Strip-farming checks soil blowing. Numerous other technical shifts in tillage and cropping methods are advocated.

Native pastures which it was feared might be permanently dead are also being revived. Moisture conservation again! Contour furrows are plowed at wide intervals around the slopes of the grass lands, and the rainfall is caught and delivered to the roots of the grama and buffalo sod. Recovery has been surprising. Gradually the raw scars are healed by grass, but the furrows and ridges remain—a permanent trap for the dashing rains.

> "The greenest, most productive lands I saw in the dust bowl were the Soil Conservation projects."

## Witnessing the Results

Controversy still rages over some of these new methods. Ray Throckmorton, for example, believes that in most cases cropland terraces are unnecessary, that contour furrows alone usually will do the job. Terraces are pretty expensive for the farmer who is not in one of the demonstrational areas and must pay the cost out of his own pocket. Also, many farmers complain that they are having difficulty getting their broad, heavy power implements over the terraces.

Bill Baker, the gaunt, scholarly old county farm agent of Cimarron County, Oklahoma, who has won the plaudits of archaeologists for his research on the prehistoric peoples of the Southwest, told me that the farmers in his county have not had particularly good luck with contour farming. He prefers the basin lister—or damming lister, as it is sometimes called—a new tillage implement which kicks out small earthen dams across the furrows, at intervals of eight or ten feet. The little basins thus created catch and hold the rains, much as contour furrows do.

The fact remains that the greenest, most productive lands I saw in the dust bowl were the Soil Conservation projects. In some cases, virtually the entire project area of 25,000 acres was so well protected by cover crops that soil blowing will be negligible during the coming winter and spring.

> It takes money to change the character of farming throughout a whole region.

At Liberal, Kansas, I met Lloyd I. Lambert, a successful farmer. This year the rains happened to hit his land at the right time, and he harvested 850 acres of wheat. One field of 320 acres lay within the Liberal Soil Conservation project and was terraced and farmed on the contour. It yielded 17½ bushels to the acre. On the remaining 530 acres— where soil characteristics and rainfall were identical— Lambert farmed in the conventional way. His harvest from that piece averaged nine bushels. My notebook is full of similar convincing testimony. There were also occasional instances where contour farming apparently produced no appreciable results, but the evidence was preponderantly on its side.

Moisture conservation alone will not save the dust bowl. In great drought, even with the most intelligent methods, the topsoil is fried to powder and even the subsoil is parched far below the root growth. If a farmer makes his fall sowing of wheat under such conditions, unless the gods of weather are unusually kind, his fields will blow away in the spring. Farmers have long known this in a haphazard, but the land of big wheat has always been gambler's country. . . .

## Getting Needed Financial Help

It is not pure contrariness that keeps many a dust-bowl farmer from working into a more stable type of agriculture. Some of the big wheat growers, to be sure, still look forward to a return of the lush years when they harvested and sowed and went to California for the winter. Mere campers on the land, they don't want to be tied down by diversified farming. They are the fellows who have received the publicity, though they are not typical.

But it takes money to change the character of farming throughout a whole region, and the dust-bowl farmer who has any working capital left is a rare exception. The wheat drills which I saw rolling along in choking clouds of dust this autumn were run, in many cases, by men who were making a last desperate gamble. The more extensive use of cover crops implies a shift to combination farming—livestock as well as wheat—and it takes capital to get a start in cattle these days. Even contour farming costs from 6 to 10 per cent more than the conventional methods.

Time after time I heard a wistful thought expressed by men who were taking the long look ahead. "The Government," they said, "is spending vast sums on its AAA [Agricultural Adjustment Administration] subsidy program in this region, as it is elsewhere. If there were only some way to make that money really effective, if somehow it could be used to finance a permanent shift in our type of agriculture, we could go places. And we could lick the dust storms."

[Agriculture Department Dust Bowl coordinator Roy J.] Kimmel estimates that the various agricultural agencies of the Federal Government have already poured about $200,000,000 into that area, and AAA payments compose the bulk of the total. The Soil Conservation Service, for example, has spent in the dust bowl, to date, only $4,079,000. That item of $200,000,000 does not include loans of the FCA [Farm Credit Administration] or the expenditures of WPA [Works Progress Administration], PWA [Public Works Administration] and other agencies which are partly urban.

[Secretary of Agriculture Henry A.] Wallace's Triple A subsidies are granted, of course, in the name of soil conservation, and it is true that the complex provisions of the program do include several of the improved farming practices. In some counties the subsidies for cover crops and moisture conservation have been moderately effective. Elsewhere distress has been so acute that the local committees have often winked at the qualifying provisions and handed out the money. It is significant that many farmers seem to regard the Triple A subsidies, not as payments for conservation but as their proper share of the New Deal handout. They do what they have to do to qualify.

> The Soil Conservation Service believes that approximately 6,000,000 acres of the tilled land . . . should be permanently restored to grass.

## Government Land Purchases

Kimmel has been sitting in with the AAA chieftains in Washington, and he believes the 1938 program will be more resultful. The provisions do fit the region better, and are more rigid—if they are enforced.

When the Government first invaded the dust bowl, there was much talk, sometimes from high sources, that the entire area would have to be purchased with federal funds and returned to public domain. That scared the official shirts right off the backs of local chambers of commerce. Farmers saw red, and in a year or two Washington saw light.

Government men now take a conciliatory attitude. Of the 96,000,000 acres in the dust bowl, approximately 64,000,000 is still native pasture land. The Soil Conservation Service believes that approximately 6,000,000 acres of the tilled land, widely scattered over the entire area, should be permanently restored to grass. Local people are not greatly disturbed by that prospect, for nearly everyone agrees that there are certain fields which will always blow even if carefully farmed.

Ray Throckmorton's remark was typical. "Ordinarily," he said. "I don't believe in public ownership, but I don't see how we are ever to stop the dust storms unless some of that stuff is put back under cover and kept there forever. It is a job that can never be accomplished by private enterprise. Either the Government or the states will have to step in."

Kimmel agrees, in substance, with that viewpoint.

Two years ago the Farm Security Administration—at that time Resettlement—launched an ambitious program of land purchases. Subsequently, however, much of its money was doled out on New Deal schemes elsewhere. When I was in Amarillo this fall [1937], the Government had bought or accepted options on 496,591 acres of land in the dust bowl in three states. The total cost of land and improvements was $1,574,683, about three dollars an acre.

Much of this new Government domain is in grass and always has been. Thus a considerable share of the money went for land which has not been a blow hazard, and this has brought sharp criticism. . . .

A new fund of $10,000,000 has now been allotted for land purchases, and Kimmel is determined that the dust bowl's portion of the appropriation shall be used, as far as possible, to remove the most hazardous soils from production. If he has his way, that land will then be turned over to the Soil Conservation Service, which will tackle the slow job of restoring native grasses. Subsequently, it may be leased for carefully controlled grazing. . . .

## A Potential Success Story

Someday the rains will come again, and the dust bowl will drop from the headlines. If the bitter lesson of the past five years is forgotten and the days of bonanza wheat return, with no preparation for the next great drought, all the millions now going into the task of reclamation will be wasted money. And already there are evidences that forgetting is easy. Co-ordinator Kimmel told me that around Lubbock, Texas, where rainfall has been better, approximately 200,000 acres of new sod lands have been put to the plow within the past eighteen months.

For four years the New Deal has been espousing the philosophy of a supervised agriculture for America. The dust bowl seems to offer Mr. Wallace a chance to prove his case. If he can make his millions count, if he can transform a region from gambler's land to a stable agricultural country, it will be a triumph for bureaucracy.

# World War II Leads to an American Economic Boom

## *The Economist*

The following viewpoint from the British newspaper, *The Economist*, looks back at the unfolding of the Great Depression in the United States at the point in time when World War II was just beginning in Europe. The author analyzes the U.S. attitude during the Depression, describing it mostly as one of nostalgia for a lost era of prosperity. The author further discusses the recovery that occurred during the decade following the stock market crash as well as prospects for future U.S. economic growth in light of the impending war in Europe. *The Economist* was first published in September 1843 and has dealt with economic policy and other pertinent issues throughout its nearly 200 years in print.

**SOURCE.** "The American Economy, 1929–1939," *The Economist*, vol. 5023, December 2, 1939, pp. 319–320. Copyright © 1939 The Economist Newspaper Ltd. All rights reserved. Reproduced by permission of *The Economist*, conveyed through Copyright Clearance Center, Inc.

The coming of the war has impeded the due celebration of a very important anniversary: it is just a decade, these last few weeks, since the Great Wall Street Panic. It was on September 3, 1929—a doubly ominous date—that the sacred averages of common stock prices reached their "all-time high." They touched this pinnacle and fell back, but not alarmingly at first. September was nearly over before the Stock Exchange had its first bad day, before the wiseacres began to say that quite a perceptible hesitation in the upward march of paper profits was impending. Panic did not come until October 24th—the worst day the Exchange has ever known, when even United States Steel, Jupiter of this speculative Olympus, fell by 12 points in an hour. But for three weeks, starting on that day, the market saw a torrent of selling such as no market has ever had to cope with before or since, and by the time the averages reached their lowest point for the year on November 13th the wealth of the American people, on paper, had fallen by a sum almost equal to the whole British National Debt [a significant amount due to the expense of World War I].

This was the crack that ushered in the Great Depression—not its cause, certainly, but the Sarajevo[1] that precipitated it. The anniversary is one well worth celebrating, and there may be more than ironic coincidence in the dates of these autumn months of 1929 and 1939. For if the 1920's had not built such towering structures on the sand, there might have been no Great Depression. And if there had been no Great Depression, there would certainly have been no Hitler. And if there had been no Hitler. . . .

## Nostalgia for the 1920s

Essays in the hypothetical are seldom very rewarding, and there is possibly more profit in turning aside from the wider spectacle in order to examine

> Ever since 1929 public policy in the United States has been dominated by nostalgia.

what has happened to the American economy itself in this fateful decade. Ever since 1929 public policy in the United States has been dominated by nostalgia, if not for every facet of the New Era[2] which blew itself up in 1929, then at least for its busy hubbub, its appearance (at least) of prosperity, above all its certainty of a manifest and golden destiny for the United States "just around the corner." The United States is the only country which, in an economic sense, has passed through this decade with a reminiscent eye fixed, over its shoulder, on the fabulous records of the past—the only country which is producing less wealth than a decade ago. Many of the illusions of the New Era have been shattered beyond the possibility of repair and many of its ideals have turned to dust. But if any leader could show the American people the road back to 1929, he would still be the greatest prophet in the land. . . .

The Great Depression, despite its colossal dimensions, followed the orthodox course; there were three years of rapid fall and five years of not quite so rapid recovery. By 1937 most of the indices[3] were approximately back where they started. This was true not only of industrial production in general but of the two all-important industries of automobiles and steel. Employment in industries making non-durable goods was actually above 1929. The curve of the National Income at its peak in 1937 (the temporary jump in 1936 was due to the disbursement of the veterans' bonus) was only 10 per cent, below the level of 1929, and, in view of the great deflation of prices, this can be taken as a level of real income at least no lower than in the glorious days of the bull market.

## America's Economy Becomes Mature

What is remarkable about this picture, however, is not that 1937 climbed back to the 1929 level, but that the indices retreated again after once looking the 1929 figures in the eye. By 1937 the American people were eight millions

J. Howard Miller's World War II-era poster emphasized the role women played in the U.S. industrial boom while men fought abroad. (**National Archives/Time & Life Pictures/Getty Images.**)

more numerous than in 1929. Allowing for the normal secular rate of progress, the curve of recovery should have gone on rising until it was at least 15 per cent above the peak of the previous boom. The 1929 level of production meant, in 1937, not prosperity but mass unemployment. The real problem in recent American economic history is not to explain the bursting of the distended bubble of 1929, but the collapse of the recovery in 1937 before it was a bubble at all. The disappointment caused by the premature demise of the recovery movement,

> If Britain . . . has found it possible to regain a high rate of progress after a decade in the doldrums, there is no reason whatever to expect any different course of events in America.

together with the difficulty of assigning any really satisfying reason for it, have jointly given birth to the theory, of which much has been heard from the American economists in the last twelve months, that the United States is now a "mature economy," which can hardly hope to increase its rate of production above the 1929 level.

It is difficult to take this theory seriously—or to know whether its partisans themselves take it seriously. If the United States, with its vast areas, its low debt, its inexhaustible natural resources, its rising population is a mature economy, what is Great Britain? And yet our "decadent" economy has contrived, during the decade when America was standing still, to go ahead as fast as on the average of the great Victorian era of expansion. Ten years ago the *per capita* National Income of the United States was one-third larger than the British; today it is probably no larger at all. The peculiar significance of this comparison lies in the fact that the British economy, before its recent spurt, seemed to be as completely becalmed as the American is now. In the 1920's it was Britain that stood still while other nations went ahead; in the 1930's America has taken the position we vacated. If Britain, inherently much the more "mature" of the two, has found it possible to regain a high rate of progress after a decade in the doldrums, there is no reason whatever to expect any different course of events in America.

## Assigning Blame for the Lack of Economic Growth in America

The evidence for the "maturity" theory is taken from the fact that the volume of new capital investment in America has now for a decade been well below the level that the country's inherent capacity to save could finance.

It is undeniably true that the capital industries have never been well occupied since 1929, except for the briefest of intervals in 1937. The American economy seems to have forgotten, for the moment, how to grow. But the probable explanation of this economic anæmia is to be found, not in any arrival at "maturity," but rather in the existence of institutional obstructions to a free flow of capital. Each side of the political battle accuses the other of having erected these barricades, and both are probably right. The New Deal [policies of President Franklin Roosevelt implemented in response to the Depression] has not created an atmosphere conducive to the risking of capital, while Big Business has been too slow to realise that the presence of a Democrat in the White House does not automatically preclude the earning of profits. And the Trade Unions, in their quest for higher incomes and shorter hours, have pushed the cost of labour to a level at which the working-man can hardly afford to employ himself. All these factors in combination have produced a psychological *impasse* [deadlock] in which there is insufficient capital investment because profits are inadequate, and profits are low because investment is scanty. Perhaps the severest indictment of the New Dealers is that they have frittered away the Federal Government's capacity to lead the country out of this *impasse*. Their monetary policy has already generated a colossal inflation of bank credit—which is lying unused. Budget deficits are so much a permanent arrangement that their chief significance now lies in the deflation they would cause if the Budget were balanced rather than in the inflation they cause by continuing. Neither banking policy nor deficit financing is now available to give a fresh impetus to the national economy.

> "The contemplation of a Europe that is, for the second time in a generation, tearing itself to pieces has already noticeably restored Americans' faith in their own political system."

## The War Boom

It may be, however, that a *deus ex machina*[4] arrived on the tenth anniversary of the stock market's all-time high. . . . America is having a war boom. The logical basis for it is slender enough, for the business that America will lose by her Neutrality Act[5] seems likely to be as large as what she will gain. The war boom, paradoxically enough, is based almost entirely on peaceful domestic buying. But if there is little logic behind the new boom, there is plenty of sound psychology. Wars notoriously breed sellers' markets and rising prices. It is a time to buy; it is imprudent not to buy while you can . . . the echo is unmistakable.

The contemplation of a Europe that is, for the second time in a generation, tearing itself to pieces has already noticeably restored Americans' faith in their own political system. More than possibly it will do the same for their confidence in the ability of the American economy to reach new peaks of prosperity—and, doubtless, of speculation too—which will finally remove the tang of nostalgia from the memory of 1929.

### Notes

1. Any small event that starts a dramatic chain reaction, such as the assassination of Austrian Archduke Franz Ferdinand in Sarajevo, which resulted in the start of World War I.
2. The New Era was the period of U.S. history from 1920–1929 when the country experienced economic growth and prosperity.
3. Indices are measures used to determine the health of an economy, such as income, employment rate, and commodity prices.
4. A Latin phrase that literally means "god from the machine," but refers to a plot device in fiction or theater where an improbable solution to a problem comes unexpectedly.
5. The Neutrality Act was passed by the U.S. Congress in the 1930s to keep the country from becoming involved in the increasingly tumultuous situation in Europe that eventually became World War II.

# CHAPTER 2

# Controversies Surrounding the Great Depression

# President Hoover's Interventionist and Protectionist Policies Caused the Depression

## Amity Shlaes

President Herbert Hoover has been widely criticized throughout history for his inaction in combating the forces driving the Great Depression, such as unemployment, falling wages, plummeting agricultural prices, and stock market instability. Amity Shlaes presents a revisionist view of history in the following viewpoint, arguing that it was not Hoover's inaction that worsened the Depression, but rather his overzealous policy making, interventionism, and protectionism. Shlaes contends that Hoover made three fundamental mistakes that lengthened the Depression and increased its severity—he interfered with business, signed the Smoot-Hawley tariff into law, and attempted to regulate the stock market. She claims both business and the stock market

Photo on previous page: Historians differ on what role U.S. President Herbert Hoover played in the onset of the Great Depression. (**AP Images.**)

---

**SOURCE.** Amity Shlaes, *The Forgotten Man*. New York: HarperCollins, 2007. Copyright © 2007 by Amity Shlaes. All rights reserved. Reproduced by permission of HarperCollins Publishers Inc, and the author.

are subject to natural fluctuations, and that Hoover's policies stifled the natural recovery that had in the past occurred following similar economic downturns. Amity Shlaes writes a nationally syndicated column about political economics and taxes and contributes to *Marketplace*, the National Public Radio show analyzing current economic topics.

On Wall Street, many investors were losing their livelihood [following the October 1929 stock market crash]. Most famous was the pair of men who committed suicide by leaping out of the window while holding hands: they had maintained a joint account. This was the kind of anecdotal tragedy that would come to be symbolic of the crash. But the despair was not uniform: indeed, on November 13, 1929, the city's [New York City] chief medical officer reported that there had been forty-four suicides in the preceding four weeks in Manhattan, nine fewer than the fifty-three for the same period in 1928. As for banks, some were failing, but the rate was not outside the norm for the 1920s. Total commercial bank failures for 1929 would be lower than the same statistic for 1924, 1926, or 1927.

> "The more Hoover thought about it, the more he . . . liked the idea of a war against inflation."

The nation's first impulse was correct. Washington might not have needed to do much. The miracle of the 1920s had followed a rough downturn at the start of the decade, and then a comeback. Such crashes—or panics, as they were known—did not make a lengthy slump an inevitability. Perhaps all that was needed now was for owners to sell their holdings, so that the market could find its own bottom. This was what [then Secretary of the Treasury Andrew W.] Mellon would mean when he recommended that stockholders, banks, and farmers liquidate their holdings. The phrase "to liquidate" sounded harsh, but it also represented an old and important argument. Uncertainty was one of the market's problems. Only when stocks or wages were "marked to market" and found their bottom could they rise again. . . .

## The Impulse to Intervene

As more bad news arrived, Fed officials [U.S. Federal Reserve officials], Mellon, [President Herbert] Hoover, and many others began to reconsider. After all, they reflected, an adult who had begun watching the market in 1907 had had to wait two full decades for the Dow[1] to double, until 1927. . . . In 1927, the Dow Jones Industrial Average crossed the 200 mark. Yet from the 200 of the spring of 1927 it moved to 381—nearly doubling again—by the summer of 1929. This increase seemed too steep not to be somehow economically and morally suspect. Perhaps the country was indeed in the throes of a dangerous inflation. . . .

The more Hoover thought about it, the more he too liked the idea of a war against inflation. Market fever was in any case the sort of thing Hoover deplored; he had been complaining about abuse of credit for four years [during his tenure as Secretary of Commerce under President Calvin Coolidge]. Meanwhile, the market was beginning to look worse. Not merely the margin sellers but also the regular players were suffering on Wall Street. In the fall of 1929 the Dow's new utility index plunged as well. One night in November, Robert Searle, president of the Rochester Gas and Electric Corporation, gassed himself to death after confronting more than a million in losses in a month. The death seemed a metaphor for the failing of the utilities industry, all the more so because Searle had started out as Thomas Edison's office boy. . . .

## Damaging Policies on Three Fronts

Right away—in November 1929—Hoover pushed to expand an existing public buildings program by the

General Motors president and chairman Alfred P. Sloan, Jr. was among the corporate chiefs pressured by President Hoover to keep Depression-era wages high. **(Leonard McCombe/Time & Life Pictures/Getty Images.)**

healthy sum of $423 million on the theory that the spending would boost the economy. In Washington, builders put up great structures—a new agriculture department, for example. He asked his secretary of commerce, the man who held his old job, to establish a national system of cooperation among the states in public works projects. When Congress convened in December, the president called for "the expansion of the merchant marine, the regulation of inter-State distribution of electric power, the consolidation of railroads, the development of public health services, and departmental reorganization for greater economy."

But this was only the beginning. This time, he thought, perhaps the president could broker the recovery. "Words are not of any great importance in times of economic disturbance," he announced. "It is action that counts." The problem with the economy, at least as it was evolving, was mostly a monetary or an international one—Germany was already in depression. Yet at first Hoover focused on fixing it with domestic fiscal tools. And before a year would pass, Hoover had done damage that did matter on three fronts: by intervening in business, by signing into law a destructive tariff, and by assailing the stock market.

## Interfering with Business

First came business. Hoover believed that business spending might make a difference. He thought he might cajole or bully Main Street [referring to the general U.S. public], the industrial world, and labor leaders into pulling the economy back to recovery. Less than a month after Black Tuesday, October 29, 1929, the day of the stock market crash, on November 19, 1929, he therefore called a conference of railroad presidents in the cabinet room of the White House. Railroads mattered: they were at the time still the principal means of transport for both people and goods across the nation. The president asked the executives to sustain construction. Mellon came to the meeting. Later that week, industry leaders announced they planned a full billion dollars in outlays—an amount equal to more than a third of what the federal government had spent on all its budgeted projects in 1929.

Two days later, November 21, the cabinet room was the site of another meeting, this time of leaders from big industries. The guests included Treasury secretary Mellon, again, Henry Ford, Julius Rosenwald of Sears, Pierre Du Pont, Alfred Sloan Jr. of General Motors, and Julius Barnes, who was chairman of the board of the U.S. Chamber of Commerce. After hearing their views, Hoover did something radical. He noted that "liquidation" (layoffs) had accompanied all previous American recessions and that the federal government had allowed those liquidations to take place. This time "his every instinct" told him things must be different; wages must stay in place. Otherwise values would be "stepped down"; industry must help to "cushion down" the situation. At the worst, businesses in trouble might reduce hours to share jobs. But the general push must be to keep high wages and keep up employment. . . .

> The president was, essentially, requiring that companies take the hit in profits instead of employment.

## Hoover's Policies Harm Business

Hoover's wage ideas sounded good to some. And they were indeed the opposite of federal policies in the last downturn. But they did not really make sense: to force business to go on spending when it did not want to was to hurt business. And in some areas—wages, especially—the president's policy was dramatically counterproductive. As the crash continued, profits began to drop. Yet businesses could not adjust: if they wanted to be good citizens, they had to keep their pledge to Hoover and sustain employment and wages. The president was, essentially, requiring that companies take the hit in profits instead of employment.

Later scholars would note the effect of the new precedent: wages of those who had jobs stayed the same. But many did not keep their jobs, or lost cash by being assigned part-time work—Hoover's job sharing. This was different from 1921, when companies had been able to cover their losses by cutting wages. But there was also, of course, an effect on employers. Their wage costs forced down the value of company shares, aggravating the downturn that Hoover had vowed to fight. Hoover's humanitarian policy sent a signal nationwide: do not lower wages. In the end, businesses had to choose between lowering wages and shutting down. Often, they shut down. . . .

But Hoover proceeded, undaunted. He ordered governors to increase their public spending when possible. He also pushed for, and got, Congress to endorse large public spending projects: hospitals, bridges. The president documented meticulously all the positive responses he received from governors and senators when he asked them to increase spending. Among the telegrams came one from Franklin Roosevelt of New York, who wrote that he for his part expected to expand "much-needed construction work" in his state and that construction would be "limited only by estimated receipts from revenues without increasing taxes." By April 1930 the secretary of commerce would be able to announce that public works spending was at its highest level in five years. At the same time, Hoover went to work on another front: farm prices. These were at painful lows, in part because of production incentive programs advanced by Hoover himself earlier in the decade. The government had lured farmers into overproduction.

## The Dangerous Protectionist Tariff

There was a monetary element to the problem as well. Looser money or credit policies could have limited the farmers' problems. So in fact could have more orthodox adherence to the gold standard—giving up sterilization [stabilizing the value of the dollar with the sale of U.S. securities]. But Hoover chose to stick to the narrow challenge of price without regard to monetary factors. If farm prices were too low, he would raise them. Strengthening protection might bring them up. Protectionism had in any case been part of the Republican Party platform in

1928, in which the party had reaffirmed the tariff as a "fundamental and essential principle of the economic life of this nation." And on April 15, 1929, well before the autumn siege, the president had as good as promised a new agricultural tariff: "Such a tariff not only protects the farmer in our domestic market, but also stimulates him to diversify his crop."

Now, with farmers in need, the tariff idea gained momentum. Lawmakers pushed for it. In the House, the leader was Willis Hawley of Oregon; in the Senate, Reed Smoot of Utah. In the end the legislation called for one of the highest tariffs in U.S. history. The new law made sense on an emotional level: America was in trouble, so America's domestic producers must be protected with fresh advantage. In the autumn of 1929 it became clear that a large new tariff would indeed pass the Congress— and that it would be up to Hoover whether to sign it.

> A new tariff would shut U.S. sellers off from the world at a time when they badly needed customers.

Still, for the general economy the tariff was bad news. As Benjamin Anderson of Chase Bank would point out in an address the next March [1930], the preceding fifteen years, going back to 1914, had seen an excess of exports over imports of $25 billion. America sold more than it bought in the international arena. Others agreed. A new tariff would shut U.S. sellers off from the world at a time when they badly needed customers. It would deprive foreign governments of trade. It would drive the prices of imports up for consumers at home. It would hurt other nations, nations that the United States hoped would become its markets. It would certainly hurt the worker. It would also, in the long run, hurt the farmer, by offering yet more—and greater—incentives to continue doing something that was uneconomical. . . .

## The Hooveresque Middle Ground

The medicine ball was in Hoover's hands, and this time, he dropped it. He announced that it was nationally important to have a tariff, and also important for the executive to play a key strategic role in formulating it. He wanted to stop "congressional logrolling"—the congressional game of setting tariffs on specific industries to please specific constituencies.

The position he therefore ended up adopting was Hooveresque. He would not oppose the new tariff but would battle to make it fairer. He therefore advocated the engineering of a "flexible tariff" that would be controlled by a bipartisan commission made up of a precise fifty-fifty breakdown of commissioners from each party. The commission would achieve an important goal of Hoover's: they would take tariffs as far away from politicians as he could get them. It would be a "definite rate-making body acting through semi-judicial methods." The commission would then set tariffs based on a rational review of costs and prices at home and abroad. There was one other thing: the executive would then have the authority "to promulgate or veto the conclusions of the commission." The progressive and engineer in him triumphed over the international merchant.

Congress gave Hoover what he wanted. Hoover not only signed the legislation; he signed it ceremoniously, in June 1930, using six gold pens, one each for the Republican lawmakers Smoot, [James] Watson, [Samuel] Shortridge, Hawley, [Allen] Treadway, and [Isaac] Bacharach. But by focusing on winning the battle of flexible tariffs, Hoover lost the more important struggle: to right the ship in a storm.

## International Retaliation for the Tariff

For the economists proved right: Smoot-Hawley provoked retaliatory protectionist actions by nations all over the globe, depriving the United States of markets and sending the country into a deeper slump. Dozens of nations acted, as it became clear the tariff would become law, or after the formal signature. France imposed an auto tariff; so did Italy. Australia and India legislated new duties. Canada raised tariffs three times. The first tariff, an emergency retaliation, hit 125 classes of U.S. products. The Swiss, furious at a duty on watches, boycotted U.S. imports to their country.

> " What the stock market at that moment needed was clear rules and pricing. "

There were indirect international consequences as well. Foreign governments still owed considerable debts to the United States. Some of those debts were denominated in gold. To get the gold to pay those debts, the governments and their people had to be able to sell in the United States. The tariffs made this necessary task more difficult. At a time when the country could have pulled itself out of a slump through trade, Washington was buttressing the walls preventing that trade.

## Stifling Stock Market Recovery with Policy

But this was not all. Hoover was also intervening on a third front: markets. What the stock market at that moment needed was clear rules and pricing, Mellon's "liquidation." This was what everyone expected in any case, for at that time Washington did not regulate the stock market; the exchange was a New York corporation.

Still, Hoover could scold, and he did. In his first annual message to Congress, delivered in December 1929, Hoover railed against the "wave of uncontrolled speculation" that he saw as a cause of the crash. Over the course of the winter and the next year he would speak out, too, against short selling. In a short sale, a trader borrows a stock and sells it at a certain price, in the hopes that by the time he must deliver the stock, he can buy it himself even more cheaply. Hoover believed that this was not logic but roulette at its worst. The game was dangerous because it moved away from the value of the underlying asset—shares in a company—and into the racy world of betting. Without short contracts, he reckoned, the stock market would not experience such violent ructions. The shorts, to his mind, put downward pressure on a market that might in some instances otherwise do fine. Now he wanted new rules to limit shorting.

But the argument against shorting had a flaw. For every short seller—the man who was exerting the downward pressure—there was always a long buyer—the man who bet he could get the stock for cheap under the arrangement, and then sell it himself, for more. . . .

Hoover had attacked a practice—speculative short selling—not a person. Congress was less conceptual. Legislators took the president's signal to mean they were free to turn on Wall Streeters. From the winter of 1929, they made short sellers and speculators generally targets for investigations, prosecutions, ridicule, and shame. Hoover believed that the regulation of this problem still remained with the stock exchanges and the states where they were located, but pressured the exchanges into suppressing "illegitimate speculation." Though no new law on this issue passed, the sense that the market would not be left alone to right itself disturbed investors. After rising early in 1930, the market was drifting downward, passing below 200 in October.

## Note

1. The Dow Jones Industrial Average is a stock market index reflecting the value of the largest publicly owned companies.

# President Hoover's Lack of Policy Intervention Worsened the Depression

**William E. Leuchtenburg**

In the decades following the Great Depression, many historians portrayed Herbert Hoover as a "do-nothing president" whose administration's policies, or lack thereof, failed to halt the financial crisis or alleviate public suffering. William E. Leuchtenburg concurs with this opinion in the following viewpoint and argues that while Hoover attempted to stop the Depression at its start, as the crisis progressed, the president failed to implement a successful policy to ease the suffering of Americans. Leuchtenburg contends that Hoover was content to leave the business of economic relief to the private sector. According to Leuchtenburg, Hoover was reluctant to dole out federal aid to help people for fear that they would become too dependent on handouts and thus lose the spirit of determination and perseverance that defined the country. William E. Leuchtenburg is a professor of history at the University of North Carolina at Chapel Hill. He is also one of the foremost scholars on Franklin Delano Roosevelt's life and has authored books such as *Franklin D. Roosevelt and the New Deal, 1932–1940* and *The FDR Years: On Roosevelt and His Legacy.*

On Thursday, October 24, 1929, the New York Stock Exchange opened quietly, but volume was heavy and soon prices began to plunge at such a pace that the ticker could not keep up. "By eleven o'clock," [twentieth-century economist] John Kenneth Galbraith wrote later, "the market had degenerated into a wild, mad scramble to sell. By eleven-thirty the market had surrendered to blind, relentless fear." October 29, "Black Tuesday," was far worse: $30 billion in securities self-destructed. The next morning, the *New York Times* reported: "Stock prices virtually collapsed yesterday, swept downward with gigantic losses in the most disastrous trading day in the stock market's history." By mid-November, industrials were worth only half of what they had commanded ten weeks before. (Before [President Herbert] Hoover left office, blue chip U.S. Steel dropped from 262 to 21, General Motors from 92 to 8, Montgomery Ward from 138 to 4.)

## No Historical Precedent for Dealing with a Depression

A number of Hoover's predecessors had confronted financial crises, but none had left him a usable legacy. In previous depressions—from 1837 to 1894—Martin Van Buren, James Buchanan, and Ulysses S. Grant had done nothing, and Grover Cleveland had taken a hard line against aid to the unfortunate. "All communities are apt to look to government for too much," Van Buren had declared, in explaining why he was going to "refrain from suggesting to Congress any specific plan for . . . relieving mercantile embarrassments." In later years, Hoover, too, would be categorized as a "do-nothing" president. In fact, as might have been expected of a man who had been so activist a secretary of commerce, he moved with commendable alacrity to arrest the decline. . . .

Despite all the rockets being fired from the White House, though, Hoover intended to limit the role of government. The amount he requested from Congress for construction was modest, and he advised governors that the "pursuit of public works" by the states should be "energetic yet prudent." Virtually all of the responsibility for the economic health of the nation was left with corporation directors. It was not clear, however, how much leadership would come from the private sector. The National Business Survey Conference contented itself with actions such as recommending that home owners spark revival by adding on "the extra sunporch." Moreover, if the system was "fundamentally sound," there was no need to inquire why the crash had happened or whether reforms might be required.

> "Hoover believed that the country was going through a short-term recession much like that of 1921, and hence drastic remedies were not required."

## An Aversion to Federal Aid Programs

Hoover believed that the country was going through a short-term recession much like that of 1921, and hence drastic remedies were not required. Businesses continued to report year-end profits; the stock market gained several points; and, in contrast to past panics, no large bank or corporation had collapsed. Hoover has been roundly criticized for not realizing that the stock market crash signaled the onset of the Great Depression, but no one else—including liberals—had any more perception that the slump would last over a decade. At the end of 1929, the *New York Times* judged the most important news story of the year to be not the Wall Street blowup but Admiral Richard Byrd's expedition to the South Pole. The American Economic Association foresaw a brief downturn that could be beneficial. In 1930 the former chief of the War Industries Board [the World War I government agency charged with overseeing the acquisition of supplies for the war], Bernard Baruch, a Democrat who was regarded as a financial wizard, foresaw that Hoover would be "fortunate enough, before the next election, to have a rising tide and then . . . will be pictured as the great master mind who led his country out of its economic misery."

Yet even before 1929 ended, cabinet officials were expressing concern about mounting unemployment, and by the spring of 1930 breadlines were familiar sights on city sidewalks. With municipal lodging houses bursting, New York put the homeless on a barge at an East River pier so that they would have a place to sleep. In midtown Manhattan on "one gusty March day in 1930," the historian Edward Robb Ellis has written, "hungry men stood in a triple line with their backs to the wind like cattle facing away from a storm," inching toward a soup kitchen in an Episcopal church. Of the two thousand shuffling in the cold, five hundred would be turned away when food ran out. That same month, Hoover claimed that "employment has been steadily increasing."

In April, after the Census Bureau reported more than three million out of work (the figure was actually closer to four million), he shaved the total to below two million, which, he said, was normal.

Hoover never declared that prosperity was "just around the corner" (that fatuous statement came from

> "Hoover's policies toward distress . . . reflected an aversion to the omnipotent state and a belief in 'local government responsibilities.'"

the vice president, Charles Curtis), but he did refuse to face reality. In May 1930 he announced that a "great economic experiment" had "succeeded to a remarkable degree." He told the U.S. Chamber of Commerce, "We have passed the worst, and with continued effort we shall rapidly recover." When in June a delegation that included bankers as well as bishops arrived at the White House to alert him to the accelerating decline, Hoover, visibly annoyed, told them that the economy was on the upswing and the ranks of the unemployed were dwindling. "Gentlemen," he said, "you have come sixty days too late. The depression is over." . . .

## A Muted Response to the Severe Heartland Drought

For Hoover, troubles never descended singly, but in twos and threes. That summer, at the same time muted factory whistles were testing his mettle, a devastating drought of historic proportions seared much of the heartland. A Red Cross investigator reported on conditions in eastern Arkansas: "Barefoot and without decent clothes, no meal, no flour in the bin, ragged children crying from hunger . . . nothing but . . . misery . . . far worse than the Mississippi flood." As in 1927, Hoover galvanized local communities and turned to the Red Cross, though he believed that reports of suffering were grossly exaggerated. So, too, did the Red Cross, which, thinking that starving supplicants were fakers, refused to spend much of the meager fund it had.

State authorities placed the need in the range of $120 million (almost certainly an underestimate), but the Hoover administration lowered the sum for federal aid to $25 million and specified that none of it could go for food. An Arkansas congressman wanted to know why the national government "would feed Jackasses but wouldn't feed starving babies." Many found it strange that a man who had made his reputation as an almoner [one who gives alms to the poor] in the Volga region [the area in Russia along the Volga river] not many years before would scruple about providing for his fellow citizens. Hoover, said Senator Tom Connally of Texas, had asked Congress for millions to feed "hungry Bolsheviks . . . with long whiskers and wild ideas," but now denied sustenance to hungry Americans.

## Hoover Stubbornly Maintains the Status Quo

Hoover's policies toward distress—in the drought-stricken counties and across the nation—reflected an aversion to the omnipotent state and a belief in "local government responsibilities." Even more important was the tradition of private giving. Grants from Washington, he contended, would impair the character of recipients and would deny benefactors the opportunity to sacrifice. The poor, Hoover contended, could always count on their neighbors. Curiously, he was convinced that federal relief would debauch the poor, but handouts from private agencies or from local politicians would not. Hoover's hostility to federal intervention, [U.S. newspaper editor, politician, and author] William Allen White concluded, derived from "his passionate, almost bigoted, belief in America."

> Though unemployment had climbed past the five million mark, the PECE [President's Emergency Committee for Employment] did not give a penny to any local government for relief.

As the days dragged on, the inadequacy of this approach became more apparent. By autumn, cities were staggering under mounting job losses, and the countryside was devastated. At street corners across America men on the ragged edge set up stands to sell apples to passersby. . . .

Hoover, though, had small patience with appeals to set off on a different path. When the president of General Electric urged him to call a special session of Congress to "request it to issue a billion dollars of bonds . . . to allay the tragic circumstances of unemployment," Hoover was incensed. Some time later, he received an accurate accounting of why federal relief was imperative: "Communities are impotent; state governments are shot through with politics . . . ; local charities are jaded, discouraged, bankrupt, disorganized, discredited. Their task is too great. Their support is gone." Hoover could barely contain himself in drafting a response: "This nation did not grow great from feeding upon the malignant pessimist or calamity mongers or weeping men, and prosperity for all our people will not be restored by the voluble wailings of word-sobbers nor by any legislative legerdemain proposed by theorists." He decided to abbreviate this note rather than give full throat to his fury.

A bust of President Herbert Hoover is displayed at the Herbert Hoover Presidential Library and Museum. Inaction by President Hoover deepened the severity of the Great Depression. (AP Images.)

## The National Response to Hoover's Inaction

Not until October 1930—a full year after the crash—did Hoover establish a President's Emergency Committee for Employment [PECE], and its main function was not to ease hardship but to create enough impression of motion to stave off growing demands for the dole. Modeled on the committee set up in the 1921 recession, it was headed by Colonel Arthur Woods, who had been in charge of the makeshift operation then. Though unemployment had climbed past the five million mark, the PECE did not give a penny to any local government for relief. Instead,

> By the middle of 1931, the man hailed on inauguration day as the 'Great Engineer' had become the 'Great Scrooge.'

it churned out press releases with pap topics such as urging people to hire men to "spruce up" their homes. Woods did not even try to collect trustworthy statistics on the extent of joblessness and of local resources. Asked by governors to send them the committee's plan to cope with unemployment, the PECE responded that it had no plan. . . .

The country got its first opportunity to render a verdict on the president's policies in the November 1930 midterm elections, and the returns further disheartened Hoover. The administration could point out that the party in power usually loses seats in off-year contests, but that was whistling in the dark, for progressives had done well and Hoover loyalists had fared poorly. The Republicans' big majorities in Congress had been wiped out, with the GOP's [Grand Old Party] seventeen-seat advantage in the U.S. Senate reduced to one. The party also lost fifty-two seats in the House, which, when the Seventy-second Congress convened in December 1931, Democrats would control for the first time since 1919. There was one other worrisome feature. In 1928 Franklin D. Roosevelt had barely slipped into the governorship of New York State with a 250,000 vote plurality. In 1930 he won reelection by three-quarters of a million votes, immediately becoming the front-runner to oppose Hoover in the next presidential race.

## Turning a Blind Eye to Suffering

Instead of serving as an alarm siren, the election results hardened Hoover's determination to dig in his heels. When Woods strongly recommended that he ask Congress to appropriate several hundred million dollars for public works, Hoover ignored him. "The volume of construction work in the Government is already at the maximum limit warranted by financial prudence," he asserted in his December 1930 State of the Union message. "Prosperity," he declared, "cannot be restored by raids upon the public Treasury." He further incensed congressional Democrats by charging that they were "playing politics at the expense of human misery." Senator Robert F. Wagner of New York inquired what had happened to the man who had once favored public works planning for hard times.

Hoover also rejected Woods's advice to inform Congress that "our fellow citizens are facing a desperate emergency," with "our industrial system . . . in a grave, tragic, stupid and anomalous situation." Expressing pride that "local communities through their voluntary agencies have assumed the duty of relieving individual distress and are being generously supported by the public," Hoover said that there was "minimum actual suffering." . . .

The year 1931 also saw rising anger at the president's attitude toward relief. Hoover continued to insist that communities were caring admirably for the impoverished at a time when over a million Americans were seeking refuge in freight cars—named derisively "Hoover Pullmans"— and when regiments living from hand to mouth were building shelters of scrap in empty lots in big cities— miserable shantytowns named "Hoovervilles." . . .

## Declarations of Hoover's Failures

By the middle of 1931, the man hailed on inauguration day as the "Great Engineer" had become the "Great Scrooge." In June, William Allen White wrote a novelist, "You bet I'll read your book. I see by the blurb that your heroine goes out west and falls in love with a mining engineer. She took an awful chance. America did that not long ago and now look at her." A month later, the White House correspondent of the *New York Times*, Arthur Krock, concluded: "Mr. Hoover thus far has failed as a party leader. He has failed as an economist. . . . He has failed as a business leader. . . . He has failed as a personality because of awkwardness of manner and speech and lack of mass magnetism."

During this spring, Hoover's agricultural program—the showpiece of his 1929 initiatives—ended in fiasco. Over the previous year the Grain Stabilization Corporation had been buying wheat, only to find that prices continued to tumble and that it was stuck with a huge store it could not readily dispose of. Purchasing cotton had a similar outcome; prices skidded from 17½¢ to 8¢—with no way to deal with a huge glut because Hoover refused to sanction production controls. The board eventually reached the point of urging growers to plow under every third row of cotton, but, as the historian Albert Romasco later wrote, "Despite the Farm Board's exertions to . . . sow among farmers the seeds of the new individualism, it succeeded in reaping only thistles and thorns." . . .

## Only One Man Left to Blame

After the short session of Congress ended, Hoover turned aside pleas to bring legislators back, even though the Depression was worsening. "I do not propose to call an extra session of Congress," he announced in May [1931]. "I know of nothing that would so disturb the healing process now undoubtedly going on. . . . We cannot legislate ourselves out of a world economic depression." To believe that congressional action could speed recovery, Hoover told an Indianapolis gathering in June, resembled thinking that one could "exorcise a Caribbean hurricane by statutory law." So with Congress away from March 4 to December 7, 1931, Hoover assumed full responsibility for coping with hard times—and for all that went wrong.

# Government Involvement Is Essential To Reviving the Struggling Economy

### Franklin D. Roosevelt

Between 1933 and 1935, President Franklin D. Roosevelt ushered in a series of economic initiatives designed to arrest the decline of wages, the collapse of business, and the rise in unemployment. Collectively called the New Deal, these programs allowed government restructuring of the economy, including the setting of standards for business practices— such as maximum work hours and minimum wages—and the reconstitution of banks so that their funds were secured and overseen by the U.S. Treasury. In addition, the administration created public works projects to put idle Americans to work. The U.S. economy improved somewhat in the mid-1930s. Then, in 1937, the nation's economic recovery faltered, resulting in a recession. In the following viewpoint, President Roosevelt

SOURCE. Franklin D. Roosevelt, "April 14, 1938, Address of Franklin D. Roosevelt," Essential Speeches, 2009.

describes the causes of the setback and outlines the initiatives presented to Congress for correcting it. He informs the nation's radio audience that the programs are not cheap; in fact, they will be more costly than the administration initially revealed. But he ensures the public that the return on the investment will bring the country back to prosperity.

Five months have gone by since I last spoke [in 1937] to the people of the Nation about the state of the Nation.

I had hoped to be able to defer this talk until next week because, as we all know, this is Holy Week [the week of Easter Sunday, 1938]. But what I want to say to you, the people of the country, is of such immediate need and relates so closely to the lives of human beings and the prevention of human suffering that I have felt that there should be no delay. In this decision I have been strengthened by the thought that by speaking tonight there may be greater peace of mind and that the hope of Easter may be more real at firesides everywhere, and therefore that it is not inappropriate to encourage peace when so many of us are thinking of the Prince of Peace.

Five years ago [in 1933] we faced a very serious problem of economic and social recovery. For four and a half years that recovery proceeded apace. It is only in the past seven months that it has received a visible setback.

And it is only within the past two months, as we have waited patiently to see whether the forces of business itself would counteract it, that it has become apparent that government itself can no longer safely fail to take aggressive government steps to meet it.

This recession has not returned to us the disasters and suffering of the beginning of 1933. Your money

> I conceive the first duty of government is to protect the economic welfare of all the people in all sections and in all groups.

in the bank is safe; farmers are no longer in deep distress and have greater purchasing power; dangers of security speculation have been minimized; national income is almost 50% higher than it was in 1932; and government has an established and accepted responsibility for relief.

## Government Must Be Involved in Recovery

But I know that many of you have lost your jobs or have seen your friends or members of your families lose their jobs, and I do not propose that the Government shall pretend not to see these things. I know that the effect of our present difficulties has been uneven; that they have affected some groups and some localities seriously but that they have been scarcely felt in others. But I conceive the first duty of government is to protect the economic welfare of all the people in all sections and in all groups. I said in my Message opening the last session of the Congress that if private enterprise did not provide jobs this spring, government would take up the slack—that I would not let the people down. We have all learned the lesson that government cannot afford to wait until it has lost the power to act.

Therefore, my friends, I have sent a Message of far-reaching importance to the Congress. I want to read to you tonight certain passages from that Message, and to talk with you about them.

In that Message I analyzed the causes of the collapse of 1929 in these words: "over-speculation in and over-production of practically every article or instrument used by man . . . millions of people, to be sure, had been put to work, but the products of their hands had exceeded the purchasing power of their pocketbooks. . . . Under the inexorable law of supply and demand, supplies so overran demand that production was compelled to stop. Unemployment and closed factories resulted. Hence the tragic years from 1929 to 1933."

Today I pointed out to the Congress that the national income—not the Government's income but the total of the income of all the individual citizens and families of the United States—every farmer, every worker, every banker, every professional man and every person who lived on income derived from investments—that national income had amounted, in the year 1929, to eighty-one billion dollars. By 1932 this had fallen to thirty-eight billion dollars. Gradually, and up to a few months ago, it had risen to a total, an annual total, of sixty-eight billion dollars—a pretty good come-back from the low point.

I then said this to the Congress:

But the very vigor of the recovery in both durable goods and consumers' goods brought into the picture early in 1937, a year ago, certain highly undesirable practices, which were in large part responsible for the economic decline which began in the later months of that year. Again production had outrun the ability to buy.

There were many reasons for this over-production. One of them was fear—fear of war abroad, fear of inflation, fear of nation-wide strikes. None of these fears have been borne out. . . .

Production in many important lines of goods outran the ability of the public to purchase them, as I have said. For example, through the winter and spring of 1937 cotton factories in hundreds of cases were running on a three-shift basis, piling up cotton goods in the factory, (and) goods in the hands of middle men and retailers. For example, also, automobile manufacturers not only turned out a normal increase of finished cars, but encouraged the normal increase to run into abnormal figures, using every known method to push their sales. This meant, of course, that the steel mills of the Nation ran on a twenty-four hour basis, and the tire companies and cotton factories and glass factories and others speeded up to meet the same type of abnormally stimulated demand. Yes, the buying power of the Nation lagged behind.

Thus by the autumn of 1937, last autumn, the Nation again had stocks on hand which the consuming public could not buy because the purchasing power of the consuming public had not kept pace with the production.

During the same period . . . the prices of many vital products had risen faster than was warranted. . . . For example, copper—which undoubtedly can be produced at a profit in this country for from ten to twelve cents a pound—was pushed up and up to seventeen cents a pound. The price of steel products of many kinds was increased far more than was justified by the increased wages of steel workers. In the case of many commodities the price to the consumer was raised well above the inflationary boom prices of 1929. In many lines of goods and materials, prices got so high in the summer of 1937 that buyers and builders ceased to buy or to build. . . .

The economic process of getting out the raw materials, putting them through the manufacturing and finishing processes, selling them to the retailers, selling them to the consumer, and finally using them, got completely out of balance. . . .

The laying off of workers came upon us last autumn and has been continuing at such a pace ever since that all of us, Government and banking and business and workers, and those faced with destitution, recognize the need for action.

All of this I said to the Congress today and I repeat it to you, the people of the country tonight.

I went on to point out to the Senate and the House of Representatives that all the energies of government and business must be directed to increasing the national income, to putting more people into private jobs, to giving security and a feeling of security to all people in all walks of life.

## Government Programs Will Make the Public Feel More Secure

I am constantly thinking of all our people—unemployed and employed alike—of their human problems, their human problems of food and clothing and homes and education and health and old age. You and I agree that security is our greatest need—the chance to work, the opportunity of making a reasonable profit in our business—whether it be a very small business or a larger one—the possibility of selling our farm products for enough money for our families to live on decently. I know these are the things that decide the well-being of all our people.

> I repeated to the Congress today that neither it nor the Chief Executive can afford 'to weaken or destroy great reforms which, during the past five years, have been effected on behalf of the American people.'

Therefore, I am determined to do all in my power to help you attain that security and because I know that the people themselves have a deep conviction that secure prosperity of that kind cannot be a lasting one except on a basis of fair business dealing and a basis where all from the top to the bottom share in the prosperity. I repeated to the Congress today that neither it nor the Chief Executive can afford "to weaken or destroy great reforms which, during the past five years, have been effected on behalf of the American people. In our rehabilitation of the banking structure and of agriculture, in our provisions for adequate and cheaper credit for all types of business, in our acceptance of national responsibility for unemployment relief, in our strengthening of the credit of state and local government, in our encouragement of housing, and slum clearance and home ownership, in our supervision of stock exchanges and public utility holding companies and the issuance of new securities, in our provision for social security itself, the electorate of America wants no backward steps taken. . . ."

I came to the conclusion that the present-day problem calls for action both by the Government and by the people, that we suffer primarily from a failure of consumer demand because of lack of buying power. Therefore it is up to us to create an economic upturn. . . .

## The Plan for Recovery

I went on in my Message today to propose three groups of measures and I will summarize my recommendations.

First, I asked for certain appropriations which are intended to keep the Government expenditures for work relief and similar purposes during the coming fiscal year that begins on the first of July [1938], keep that going at the same rate of expenditure as at present. That includes additional money for the Works Progress Administration; additional funds for the Farm Security Administration; additional allotments for the National Youth Administration, and more money for the Civilian Conservation Corps, in order that it can maintain the existing number of camps now in operation.

These appropriations, made necessary by increased unemployment, will cost about a billion and a quarter dollars more than the estimates which I sent to the Congress on the third of January last [1938].

Second, I told the Congress that the Administration proposes to make additional bank reserves available for the credit needs of the country. About one billion four hundred million dollars of gold now in the Treasury will be used to pay these additional expenses of the Government, and three-quarters of a billion dollars of additional credit will be made available to the banks by reducing the reserves now required by the Federal Reserve Board.

These two steps taking care of relief needs and adding to bank credits are in our best judgment insufficient by themselves to start the Nation on a sustained upward movement.

Therefore, I came to the third kind of Government action which I consider to be vital. I said to the Congress:

> You and I cannot afford to equip ourselves with two rounds of ammunition where three rounds are necessary. If we stop at relief and credit, we may find ourselves without ammunition before the enemy is routed. If we are fully equipped with the third round of ammunition, we stand to win the battle against adversity.

> "In recommending this [recovery] program I am thinking not only of the immediate economic needs of the people of the Nation, but also of their personal liberties. . . . I am thinking of our democracy."

This third proposal is to make definite additions to the purchasing power of the Nation by providing new work over and above the continuing of the old work.

First, to enable the United States Housing Authority to undertake the immediate construction of about three hundred million dollars worth of additional slum clearance projects.

Second, to renew a public works program by starting as quickly as possible about one billion dollars worth of needed permanent public improvements in our states, and their counties and cities.

Third, to add one hundred million dollars to the estimate for Federal aid highways in excess of the amount that I recommended in January.

Fourth, to add thirty-seven million dollars over and above the former estimate of sixty-three million for flood control and reclamation.

Fifth, to add twenty-five million dollars additional for Federal buildings in various parts of the country.

In recommending this program I am thinking not only of the immediate economic needs of the people of the Nation, but also of their personal liberties—the most precious possession of all Americans. I am thinking of

our democracy. I am thinking of the recent trend in other parts of the world away from the democratic ideal.

## America Must Preserve Democracy

Democracy has disappeared in several other great nations—disappeared not because the people of those nations disliked democracy, but because they had grown tired of unemployment and insecurity, of seeing their children hungry while they sat helpless in the face of government confusion, government weakness—weakness through lack of leadership in government. Finally, in desperation, they chose to sacrifice liberty in the hope of getting something to eat. We in America know that our own democratic institutions can be preserved and made to work. But in order to preserve them we need to act together, to meet the problems of the Nation boldly, and to prove that the practical operation of democratic

President Franklin Roosevelt—depicted here in a bronze sculpture by Robert Graham in Washington, DC—put key initiatives in place to restore the U.S. economy. (Brendan Smialowski/Getty Images.)

government is equal to the task of protecting the security of the people.

Not only our future economic soundness but the very soundness of our democratic institutions depends on the determination of our Government to give employment to idle men. The people of America are in agreement in defending their liberties at any cost, and the first line of that defense lies in the protection of economic security. Your Government, seeking to protect democracy, must prove that Government is stronger than the forces of business depression. . . .

We are a rich Nation; we can afford to pay for security and prosperity without having to sacrifice our liberties into the bargain.

In the first century of our republic we were short of capital, short of workers and short of industrial production, but we were rich, very rich in free land, and free timber and free mineral wealth. The Federal Government of those days rightly assumed the duty of promoting business and relieving depression by giving subsidies of land and other resources.

> It is going to cost something to get out of this recession . . . but the profit of getting out of it will pay for the cost several times over.

Thus, from our earliest days we have had a tradition of substantial government help to our system of private enterprise. But today the Government no longer has vast tracts of rich land to give away and we have discovered, too, that we must spend large sums of money to conserve our land from further erosion and our forests from further depletion. The situation is also very different from the old days, because now we have plenty of capital, banks and insurance companies loaded with idle money; plenty of industrial productive capacity and many millions of workers looking for jobs. It is following tradition as well as necessity, if Government strives to put idle money and idle men to work, to increase our public wealth and to build up the health and strength of the people—to help our system of private enterprise to function again.

## Increased Spending Will Soon Result in Increased Profits

It is going to cost something to get out of this recession this way but the profit of getting out of it will pay for the cost several times over. Lost working time is lost money. Every day that a workman is unemployed, or a machine is unused, or a business organization is marking time, it is a loss to the Nation. Because of idle men and idle machines this Nation lost one hundred billion dollars between 1929 and the Spring of 1933, in less than four years. This year you, the people of this country, are making about twelve billion dollars less than you were last year.

If you think back to the experiences of the early years of this Administration you will remember the doubts and fears expressed about the rising expenses of Government. But to the surprise of the doubters, as we proceeded to carry on the program which included Public Works and Work Relief, the country grew richer instead of poorer.

It is worthwhile to remember that the annual national people's income was thirty billion dollars more last year in 1937 than it was in 1932. It is true that the national debt increased sixteen billion dollars, but remember that in that increase must be included several billion dollars worth of assets which eventually will reduce that debt and that many billion dollars of permanent public improvements—schools, roads, bridges, tunnels, public buildings, parks and a host of other things meet your eye in every one of the thirty-one hundred counties in the United States.

No doubt you will be told that the Government spending program of the past five years did not cause the increase in our national income. They will tell you that business revived because of private spending and investment. That is true in part, for the Government spent only a small part of the total. But that Government spending acted as a trigger, a trigger to set off private activity. That is why the total addition to our national production and national income has been so much greater than the contribution of the Government itself. In pursuance of that thought I said to the Congress today:

> I want to make it clear that we do not believe that we can get an adequate rise in national income merely by investing, and lending or spending public funds. It is essential in our economy that private funds must be put to work and all of us recognize that such funds are entitled to a fair profit. . . .

You may get all kinds of impressions in regard to the total cost of this new program, or in regard to the amount that will be added to the net national debt. It is a big program. Last autumn [1937] in a sincere effort to bring Government expenditures and Government income into closer balance, the Budget I worked out called for sharp decreases in Government spending during the coming year. But, in the light of present conditions, conditions of today, those estimates turned out to have been far too low. This new program adds two billion and sixty-two million dollars to direct Treasury expenditures and another nine hundred and fifty million dollars to Government loans—the latter sum, because they are loans, will come back to the Treasury in the future.

## Getting out of the Red

The net effect on the debt of the Government is this— between now and July 1, 1939—fifteen months away— the Treasury will have to raise less than a billion and a half dollars of new money.

Such an addition to the net debt of the United States need not give concern to any citizen, for it will return to the people of the United States many times over in increased buying power and eventually in much greater Government tax receipts because of the increase in the citizen income.

What I said to the Congress today in the close of my message I repeat to you now.

> Let us unanimously recognize the fact that the Federal debt, whether it be twenty-five billions or forty billions, can only be paid if the Nation obtains a vastly increased citizen income. I repeat that if this citizen income can be raised to eighty billion dollars a year the national Government and the overwhelming majority of state and local governments will be definitely "out of the red." The higher the national income goes the faster will we be able to reduce the total of Federal and state and local debts. Viewed from every angle, today's purchasing power—the citizens' income of today—is not at this time sufficient to drive the economic system of America at higher speed.

> Responsibility of Government requires us at this time to supplement the normal processes and in so supplementing them to make sure that the addition is adequate. We must start again on a long steady upward incline in national income.

# New Deal Policies Have Stifled the Economy

## Robert A. Taft

In the 1939 speech that follows, Robert A. Taft, a U.S. senator from Ohio and a staunch conservative critic of the New Deal, criticizes President Franklin Roosevelt's recovery plan to lift the nation out of the Great Depression. Taft expresses the opinion that the administration's experiment has been too costly and ineffective in restoring employment and encouraging market growth. He believes that the government's various attempts to provide jobs and to regulate business practices in the name of assisting the poor and unemployed have simply caused interference in the market system and created a welfare state in which idle Americans become dependent on the government for their livelihood. According to Taft, all government-run relief efforts should be temporary and should not discourage private business from getting Americans back to work. For these reasons, he insists that the nation accept that the New Deal is a failure and abandon most of its programs.

---

**SOURCE.** Robert A. Taft, "A Declaration of Republican Principles: The New Deal Tide Is Rapidly Receding," *Vital Speeches of the Day*, vol. 5, April 1, 1939, pp. 381–384. Reproduced by permission.

The Republican Party today is still the minority party, but the general impression in Washington and throughout the country is that the New Deal tide is rapidly receding, and that the people are again looking to the Republican Party for leadership. It is most important that the Republicans, even though they are still in the opposition, formulate their program on which to appeal to the people for a change of administration, and the Frank Committee[1] has been working on a declaration of Republican principles.

We find an overwhelmingly difficult problem before us. After six years of New Deal rule, after every kind of experiment, and the addition of twenty billion dollars to the national debt, the fundamental problems are still unsolved. More than ten million people are unemployed in the United States today, about three million of them receiving a bare subsistence from W.P.A. [Works Progress Administration] Twenty million people are looking to the government for food. Millions more are receiving inadequate wages, and fall in that underprivileged class for whom New Dealers have shed tears in every speech, and to whom they have repeatedly promised prosperity and security. And yet there are more people underprivileged today, more people who have barely enough to live on, or not enough to live on, than there have been at any time except at the very bottom of the depression.

> We have come out of every past depression more quickly, to a higher standard of income, and to greater employment, without measures of the New Deal character.

## The New Deal Has Failed

The national income in 1938 was not much more than sixty billion dollars. If we go back ten years, we find a national income of eighty billion dollars, and ten million fewer people among whom to divide it. The average income per individual is thirty per cent less than it was in 1928. Of course times are hard.

There can be no absolute proof that this condition has been created or prolonged by the policies of the present Administration [of Franklin D. Roosevelt], but we have come out of every past depression more quickly, to a higher standard of income, and to greater employment, without measures of the New Deal character. Certainly there is no doubt that the New Deal policies have utterly failed in their objectives.

There can be only one main purpose in any intelligent program today—that is to improve the condition of the millions of unemployed, and the other millions who are below a reasonable standard of life. If that problem cannot be solved, our whole republican form of government must admit itself a failure. When we see the conditions which exist in some of our cities, and I have seen them in Ohio as you have seen them in New York, we very quickly lose our pride in the statistics which show a higher average standard of living in the United States than elsewhere. When you see the conditions which social workers see every day, you cannot be surprised that they are eager to adopt any measure which seems to furnish direct assistance to the bitter conditions their charges face, no matter what the other consequences of those measures.

> There has been no real interest in trying to restore private industry, and the assumption has been that the government could do everything better than it was done before.

It is a problem which challenges the Yankee ingenuity of the American people, and of course we Republicans claim a little more of that Yankee ingenuity, particularly from Maine and Vermont, than is possessed by the Democrats. The New Deal must have credit for trying every possible remedy which anyone suggested, sound or unsound, and through experimentation they have eliminated a considerable number of their favorite panaceas; at least they have eliminated them in the minds of all reasonable men, even if they themselves are unwilling to abandon them.

## New Dealers Distrust Business

The New Deal is such a conglomeration of all kinds of measures that it is interesting for a moment to try to analyze just what it really is. Its objectives undoubtedly were to help the nation, and particularly the lower income groups, but from the beginning it has been motivated apparently by a complete distrust of our entire economic and business system, extending almost to every individual business man. The assumption was that because a great depression occurred, all of the former principles accepted as the cause for American leadership in the world should be discarded, and this in spite of the fact that the depression was world-wide, and affected many other nations where an entirely different business system existed. There has been no real interest in trying to restore private industry, and the assumption has been that the government could do everything better than it was done before.

This critical attitude extended to the most accepted fiscal principles, such as the belief (which has inspired every past President, Republican and Democratic), that there is a moral obligation to hold government expenses down to revenues, and conduct the United States Government on the same sound business principles which are necessary to avoid bankruptcy in private industry and ultimate repudiation by government.

The President even abandoned the sound currency ideas which have always guided the United States, devalued the dollar under the almost childish [Roosevelt financial adviser George F.] Warren theory that this would increase domestic prices, and flirted with the idea of an inflation of the currency. There is no doubt that the New Dealers have a deep-seated distrust of the entire system of individual initiative, free competition, and reward for hard work, ingenuity and daring, which have made America what it is.

## Government Takes Control

They have relied on three types of government activity. The first type consists of direct relief, in different forms, to the lower income groups. Beginning with assistance to the States, which were building up a very satisfactory method of handling relief, a combination of direct and work relief under public-spirited citizen boards, cooperating with private agencies, the New Deal suddenly decided that no one could do the job as well as they could, and as a condition of the financial assistance which was necessary, insisted on complete administrative control. Finding this too much of a job, they returned the unemployables to the States, and undertook to provide work relief for all employables. That job has never been completely done, and the expense is so tremendous that it probably never will be. The attempt to administer from Washington a great work relief program throughout the entire United States has resulted in inefficiency, politics, and a vast expense which threatens a complete bankruptcy of the federal government. Other relief measures are the C.C.C. [Civilian Conservation Corps], the N.Y.A. [National Youth Administration], the Farm Security Administration, and other minor agencies.

> No man can tell when the government may step into his business, and nullify all of the effort and energy and ingenuity he may have shown in developing that business.

The second type of New Deal activity includes the government regulatory measures, which attempt to raise the income of this group or that group by controlling prices, wages, hours and practices throughout the United States. Such were the N.R.A.

[National Recovery Administration] and the A.A.A. [Agricultural Adjustment Administration]. Such are the laws regulating agriculture today, the Guffey Coal Act, the Wage-Hour Law. This type of law has completely failed in its purpose. Farm prices are as low today as they were five and one-half years ago, before the agricultural control measures began. The administration of the Guffey Coal Act for two years has done no more than impose expense on the industry. The Wage-Hour Law threatens to drive hundreds of people out of small business, and may do more harm than good. Attempts to fix prices have been frequent in history throughout the world. Without questioning the wisdom of the purposes sought, experience has shown, as in the case of the Brazil coffee control and the East Indian rubber control, that such attempts are doomed to failure. Our own experience does not contradict that conclusion.

Furthermore, this type of law is one of the most discouraging to private enterprise. No man can tell when the government may step into his business, and nullify all of the effort and energy and ingenuity he may have shown in developing that business. He is hounded by inspectors, excessive regulation, reports, and red tape. Many have gone out of business, and many have stayed out of business because they could not feel certain that with all this government regulation they might not be utterly wasting their time and their money.

## Unprofitable Public Works Programs

The other type of New Deal experiment is direct government business activity in fields where the government thinks that private enterprise has fallen down on its job. Of this character are the T.V.A. [Tennessee Valley Authority], the Rural Electrification Administration, the lending agencies extending government credit to home owners and farm owners, the building of canals and other self-liquidating public works. Unquestionably some of this activity is justified, though usually the reason that private capital has failed to enter the field is because the enterprise is unprofitable in spite of the glowing prospectus of some government department.

But there are some unprofitable things which a government should start, and governments always have done something of this kind. It is a question of degree. It is very doubtful in my mind whether the T.V.A. ever was justified in view of the development of public utilities in the Tennessee Valley, but now we have it, and have to operate it to the best advantage. Private capital could not undertake the building of canals, but neither should the government unless they are economically sound, and justified by the tolls which can be collected.

## Creating a Welfare State

The lending of funds to stimulate the building industry under the F.H.A. [Federal Housing Administration] seems to me justified as an emergency matter. And so also the Federal Farm Loan Banks fill a need which for one reason or another private capital could not reach. In this lending field, however, the government, as far as possible, should create a set-up which can be taken over by private lending agencies under government supervision, and in general there should be no further extension of government activity and competition unless it is absolutely necessary.

I have pointed out that the New Deal seemed to be inspired with a hostility to the entire pre-existing American economic system. The result is that these three types of measures which I have described have not been administered with any special care to preserve the best features of private industry, and encourage it to bring about recovery. The relief measures have been inefficient and expensive. They have resulted in a tremendous burden of taxation, which bears down on the man who is trying to make his own living. There has been no effort

First Lady Eleanor Roosevelt (right) rides in a mine car in Bellaire, Ohio, in 1935. Regulations imposed by the Roosevelt administration imposed costs on U.S. industries such as coal mining. (**AP Images.**)

to preserve conditions under which a man, striving for a private job and doing his job well, shall be encouraged and preferred to the man on W.P.A. The other two types of measures, government regulation and government competition, have directly discouraged private activity of every kind. More men have gone out of business in the last five years than have gone into business, because of the complete uncertainty whether they can survive a constant government interference.

Now we are told that everything has changed, and the administration is going to treat business like human beings. The very adoption of a so-called policy of appeasement admits that American business men and

> I think we must recognize . . . that relief will never do more than provide a bare living, and will never be a satisfactory substitute for real work in private industry.

men who would like to go into business have been badgered and discouraged to an extent which requires an absolute reversal of government policy. Secretary [of Commerce Harry] Hopkins made a speech in Des Moines, and Secretary [of Treasury Henry] Morgenthau is having mottoes hung in the offices of the Treasury Department with the legend "Does it help recovery?"

But, as the old saying goes, "fine words butter no parsnips." The appeasement policy is like the famous "breathing spell for business," only a smoke-screen to conceal the real policies of the Administration. It cannot be sincere. Whenever any question of action arises, the President is just as determined in his previous policies as he ever has been before. . . .

## The Right Path to Correcting New Deal Abuses

What then should be the Republican program? It must combine a policy of encouragement to private industry, which can put millions of men to work, with sincere and effective administration of relief measures to assist directly the lower income groups. It must recognize the absolute necessity of relief measures in this country for many years to come. Before the great depression it was reasonable to hope that our economic system had reached a point where government help was unnecessary except in cases of misfortune. It was reasonable to hope that a man who worked diligently during his active life could provide a home and an income for his old age. But the depression of 1929 to 1932 showed us that our system had not reached that point. Even if we eliminated unemployment, the fact remains that many people must work at poor jobs, the product of which is of so little value that the rest of the population will not pay them an adequate living. And so we must assist the lower income groups by direct relief, by work relief, by old age pensions, by unemployment insurance, and by some form of housing subsidy.

But the administration of this relief must be carried on with the greatest care, that it may not destroy our entire American system, and put the whole population on relief. It must be carried on with economy, because the cost of supporting those who do not work is undoubtedly borne by those who are working. The return from capital will never support but a small proportion of the population. The greatest part of the cost of relief can only come from the income of those who are actually working, and if we impose too heavy a burden on that income, there will no longer be any incentive to work, and certainly no incentive to put other men to work.

I think we must recognize, after all, that relief will never do more than provide a bare living, sad will never be a satisfactory substitute for real work in private industry. Old age pensions can never be so high as to be a satisfactory substitute for a house and a reasonable income, saved by the effort of the family which has worked successfully. We see today that we have reached the limit of popular approval of further expenditures for W.P.A., and if we were raising by taxation our entire budget, we would find the popular opposition even stronger. And it is right that it should be so, because the burden of supporting those who do not work cannot be allowed to grow to a point at which it will discourage all initiative and all effort on the part of the other two-thirds of the population.

For the same reason, the relief agencies must be administered so that those on relief are not better off

> The people must feel again that the making of a deserved profit is not a crime, but a merit. . . . They must feel again that the government does not regard every business man as a potential crook.

than the people who are working. A man who has saved and built his home should certainly be better off than the man who has saved nothing. He should be better off than the man who has the good fortune to live in a subsidized apartment-house built by the government.

In short, in administering relief, we must recognize that it is only a palliative, only a stop-gap, and that it is not an end in itself, as many of our New Deal friends seem to think.

In the second place, we must take every possible measure to cure the unemployment problem. It can only be cured by more jobs in private industry. We must, therefore, take every possible measure to encourage people to put their time and money again into the development of private industry. We must see that there is an incentive and a reward for initiative, hard work, and persistence. The problem is partly psychological and partly practical. The people must feel again that the making of a deserved profit is not a crime, but a merit. They must feel again that the government is interested in the prosperity of the business man. They must feel again that the government does not regard every business man as a potential crook.

But there must be more than mental reassurance. There must be an abandonment as far as possible of government fixing of prices, wages, and business practices. Americans must be assured that they will not be met by government competition in their field of business activity. They must feel that government activity will be confined to keeping their markets open, free and competitive, so that they will have an equal chance with their little neighbor or their big neighbor. They must feel that government expenses will be held down as far as possible, so that the tax burdens may not deprive them of the fruits of their most successful efforts. They would like to know that the currency is stable, the government's fiscal policy sound, and all danger of inflation of the currency removed.

If we can restore business activity to the conditions which existed in 1928, we would have a national income of ninety billion dollars, nearly fifty per cent more than we have today. If it could be done then, why can't it be done now? . . .

If we can stop spending money now, if we can stop the tremendous expansion of government activity, regulation and taxation, it is not too late to resume the progress which made this country the envy of the world; but if we continue for six years more the course which we have pursued, it is a bold man who will say that we can restore then prosperity under a democratic form of government.

## Note

1. The Frank Committee was a group organized by author and educator Glenn Frank, a Republican critic of the New Deal.

# Public Ownership of Utilities Can Exist in Harmony with Private Ownership

## Arthur E. Morgan

Arthur E. Morgan argues in the following speech given in 1937 that the public—that is, government—operation of utilities is a worthwhile venture. In his opinion, creating a national electricity grid, for example, could ensure that those regions that have a dearth of power generation acquire needed electricity from those that have a surplus. In addition, Morgan believes that adopting public control would bring prices down for consumers and allay fears that private companies were price-fixing a utility needed for all aspects of modern life. Morgan, however, contends that public ownership need not—and should not—drive out private companies. Advocating that these existing companies must

**SOURCE.** Arthur E. Morgan, "Intelligent Reasonableness and the Utilities: Democratic Decency or Chronic Bitterness?" *Vital Speeches of the Day*, vol. 3, February 1, 1937, pp. 230–235. Reprinted with permission from the author Morgan Institute for Community Solutions and Faith Morgan.

be respected as viable business enterprises, he asserts that private and public utilities should work together, sharing knowledge and feeding the same national market, so that Americans receive the power they need. He believes the Tennessee Valley Authority should be the flagship government program that proves whether or not the public utility can coexist with private firms while avoiding the tendency of government operations to become inefficient, bloated bureaucracies. An educator and civil engineer, Arthur E. Morgan served as the first chairman of the Tennessee Valley Authority from 1933 to 1938.

This is an effort to state my personal views on the electric power issue, especially as it affects the Tennessee Valley Authority [TVA], and also to indicate the social attitude which leads to my conclusions. In this physical setting the power program of the TVA is part of a far-reaching project for the unified development of the Tennessee River system. The spirit in which that program is worked out will tend to reflect the personal and social outlooks of those who formulate and administer it.

In the background of the electric power controversy is the long struggle over the elimination of special privilege and the reduction of arbitrary and capricious inequalities of opportunity. No less important than equality of opportunity is the increase in total opportunity through technical developments and social organization. The electric power industry should exist for the consumer, and not primarily as a profitable field of investment or to supply business for investment bankers.

In the long run this main purpose of providing the widest and best possible service at the lowest possible cost will be most fully realized if aggressive action in the public inter-

> I believe that we should deal with the private power companies to the end of eliminating abuses, while preserving the right of the people to acquire their own power service by public ownership if they choose.

est is undertaken in a spirit of open dealing and of honest regard for legitimate interests, both public and private. In the long run sharp practice and arbitrary methods will not be helpful either to the public or to private interests.

## Cooperation Is the Key to Success

A very important decision is involved in the treatment of the power issue in TVA territory. Shall there be an effort on the part of public officials to work with the private utility companies to remove abuses, to insure maximum service at minimum cost, and to insure opportunity for public ownership where it is desired, or shall men who administer public projects drift into an attitude of a fight to the finish against the private power companies, which might have the natural and perhaps inevitable consequence of disruption of the private systems, the destruction of legitimate investments and of economical service, and the sudden, if unexpected, throwing of great power systems into premature and unprepared-for public ownership? The results of non-cooperation might have the effect of a violent public reaction against government participation in the power business.

I believe that we should deal with the private power companies to the end of eliminating abuses, while preserving the right of the people to acquire their own power service by public ownership if they choose. In the process of transition from private to public ownership there should be respect for legitimate private investments in the utility business, and individual local communities should be required to respect the interests of the larger communities of which they are a part by preserving the economy and efficiency of well-integrated power systems. I believe we should endeavor to work with the private companies on the basis of mutual confidence and good-will, but with circumspection, and without surrendering any weapons before a satisfactory settlement is reached.

I do not advocate cooperation through any naive belief that the private companies have a consistent record of good behavior, for I believe that those who advocate a fight to the finish have strong arguments in their favor. The aims of some powerful leaders in the private electric utility industry commonly have been to ruthlessly destroy public ownership by every possible means. For years the National Electric Light Association published a propaganda yearbook called "Political Ownership," which, in my opinion, failed to meet the standards of fair play and good citizenship. While president of Antioch College I was informed by the vice president and general manager of a large power company that "the least suggestion of encouragement to even mildly discuss public ownership of power would be an offense to his company. . . .

Partly by such direct personal knowledge and partly by the reports of the Federal Trade Commission and otherwise I have come to the belief that the attitude of a ruthless fight to the finish and without quarter against public ownership of power has been a characteristic position of the private utilities. I believe that in their fight private utility interests have bribed Legislatures and public utility commissioners, controlled newspapers and banks, endeavored to cripple or destroy responsible and sound educational institutions which dared to be independent, threatened college professors and others with libel if they dared to publish the facts, and perhaps have made it difficult for public ownership projects to sell bonds. . . .

Yet, notwithstanding my own experiences and what I have learned of utility abuses, I believe that at the present time the proper attitude to take with reference to TVA

The Tennessee Valley Authority's hydroelectric system, including the Clinch River's Norris Dam, still generates power alongside private utilities. (AP Images.)

power is to strive to find a basis of agreement between the TVA and the private utilities which will protect both public and private investments, and will lead to the widest possible distribution of electric power at the lowest possible rates. I believe that only in that way can we secure the greatest sum total of social values whether under public or private administration. Since the creation of the Tennessee Valley Authority I have taken that attitude. . . .

> The assumption that only political agitation and action are necessary to bring about sound public ownership of power is naive.

## Government Needs a National Power Policy

Our government has little experience in handling large operating businesses, and we have not yet developed effective methods. With all the good-will in the world, it will take time to evolve them. The assumption that only political agitation and action are necessary to bring about sound public ownership of power is naive, and will lead ultimately to higher costs and to more restricted service. There are real and difficult problems to be solved, both technical and administrative.

I favor enough public ownership to enable the country to work out effective methods on a life-sized scale, but not so much public ownership that we shall be swamped by inefficiency before we learn how to make it effective and economical. The people have a right to actual examples of public ownership to supply a basis for coming to long-time conclusions on the subject. We should not be forced to decide by abstract theory. I disagree both with private utility men who would prevent any trial of public ownership on a large scale, and with public ownership advocates who would take a course the success of which would bring the utilities to unconditional surrender.

To promote fair and consistent conditions in Federal power projects, and in accord with the President's ideas, there probably should be developed through Congressional action a national power policy, administered by a Federal agency, which will enable the people of the United States and the utility interests to predict future action and to plan accordingly. . . .

## Making Things Equitable for Public and Private Power

There should be absence of arbitrary coercion on both sides. Private companies should cease coercion in the form of obstructive litigation, inaccurate and misleading propaganda, interference with financing public ownership projects in the investment market, if such interference exists, or by bringing government into ridicule and contempt. Public officials should cease coercion, as by subsidies to duplicating and competing systems, by threats of constructing duplicating systems if arbitrarily fixed prices are not accepted, or by threats of disruption of private systems with the effect of preventing refinancing of the private companies.

> If the TVA has power over and above its own needs and the needs of all its other customers, it should sell that power to the private utilities.

Where a private distribution system is taken over by the public, the loyal and efficient employees of the private system, except those in policy forming positions, also should be taken over by the public, without loss of security of tenure.

As a part of its program for the unified development of the Tennessee River system, the TVA is building a series of great dams which inevitably will develop a very large amount of power. It would be a great economic loss for this power to be wasted while the private utilities build duplicate and competing power plants. If the TVA has power over and above its own needs and the needs of all its other customers, it should sell that power to the private utilities at about what it would cost the private utilities to generate their own power. The private utilities, on the other hand, if assured of such supply, should not build additional generating plants until that assured supply of government power is fully used.

I am of the opinion that some type of power transmission pool, as recently suggested by the President, perhaps somewhat along the lines of the British grid system, may prove to be desirable. One form of pool might be somewhat as follows:

The power pool organization would own the transmisson lines. It would not generate electricity, but would buy it from the private or TVA power plants, which would remain in their present ownership. The pool would transmit that power and sell it at wholesale to any local distribution system either publicly or privately owned. The transmission pool would buy from the cheapest sources, and would sell wherever the power was needed. This method would reduce the total amount of generating capacity necessary, for if any region needed more power than the plants in that region could supply, the shortage could be met from some other region where there was a surplus. Such a project would raise questions vital to all interested parties. Before a transmission pool could be established it would be necessary for the parties to agree on the general conditions of purchase, transmission, and sale.

## Reaching an Agreement

"Power transmission pool" is a very general term which might be applied to many types of working arrangements. At one extreme some public officials, I believe, have suggested conditions which might largely destroy the private utilities; while at the other extreme the private utilities have suggested arrangements which would seem to be contrary to sound public policy.

The great divergence in these initial proposals for a pool might be looked at as playing for position among

horse-traders. That kind of diplo-
macy leads to charges of unreason-
ableness and bad faith. I am of the
opinion that for the haggling tradition to be largely replaced in public
affairs by the policy of disinterested
appraisal and planning would represent a substantial advance in the
art of government, though in every
large issue there are elements not susceptible to close
analysis, on which judgment must be somewhat arbitrary. I have found repeatedly in public and private life
that straightforward and open approach to men of large
experience and responsibility commonly meets with
similar response, and that the bluffing and horse-trading
attitude often is a weak method of procedure. I speak
from thirty years of experience in public life in the use
of the methods of disinterested analysis and appraisal in
solving similar problems, so I am not abashed by charges
of being impractical.

> Private ownership has had grave faults, but effective public ownership methods on a large scale have yet to be developed.

If the idea of a power pool were in danger of being dis-
missed as not feasible, I believe it should be approached
by a body of disinterested and competent economists
and other qualified men who would explore it from a
non-partisan position. If the TVA and the private utilities cannot get together, the public should know from
such disinterested sources the exact reasons for failure to
reach agreement.

It is my opinion that America has not yet developed
methods and policies which would justify settling permanently upon a policy with reference to ownership and
operation of electric power facilities. The issue is not
only one of good intent but also one of solving technical,
administrative and legislative problems. At the moment
the problem may seem to be one of removing inequalities
of opportunity, but the no less important issue remains
of so developing the industry as to result in a very great

total increase of opportunity to use electric power. That result will be furthered best by cooperation rather than conflict.

Private ownership has had grave faults, but effective public ownership methods on a large scale have yet to be developed. Suddenly to add a vast business to our national government, which might be the unexpected outcome of war to the death on certain large utility systems, might discredit public ownership and set it back for a generation, or it might create another government bureaucracy without adequate controls. There are great bureaucracies which, like some utility organizations, are considerably removed from direct responsiveness to the public will.

Democracy is general participation of the people in government and sensitiveness of government to the needs of the people. It may be possible to devise forms of control and administration which will have more of the real character of democracy than would a great government bureaucracy, and without destroying the efficiency of well-integrated power systems. America has not been very creative in developing effective forms of democracy. When the power issue is finally worked out, I believe its organization may have some of the characteristics of private business and some of public business. That is the tendency in democratic Switzerland and in certain other progressive countries. In public ownership there may be combinations of local autonomy in distribution, with centralized supervision and control, and with much larger organizations for transmission and perhaps for generation of power. One reason for not rushing headlong into extensive public ownership is that we need time to work out effective methods. The TVA is excellently situated to make such a contribution.

# Public Ownership of Utilities Will Destroy Jobs

### John Fort

In the following viewpoint written in 1937, John Fort, a self-described middle-aged family man who works for a privately owned power company, fears for the security of his job as the government begins its initial foray into establishing publicly owned utilities. Fort claims that the Tennessee Valley Authority, a government project to provide electricity to parts of the South, is a pet concern of politicians trying to win votes. He asserts that this single-mindedness unfortunately disregards the livelihoods of many Americans who are employed by private power companies, which will be threatened by the regulations and imposed pricings of the government program. Fort acknowledges that government can have a role in resolving national and regional problems, but he insists that it has no business getting involved in private industry, especially when the interests of hardworking citizens are sacrificed to dubious public good.

---

**SOURCE.** John Fort, "I Work for a Power Company," *Saturday Evening Post*, vol. 210, September 11, 1937, pp. 27, 102–104. Copyright © 1937 Saturday Evening Post Society. Reproduced by permission.

I live in the South and I work for a privately owned public-utility corporation with a large invested capital, which sells electricity. I live and work in an area where my employer is directly affected by the competition of the Tennessee Valley Authority. I work for wages of less than two hundred dollars per month and more than one hundred dollars per month. I am in the white-collar class. I have a wife, three children and a small house on which there is a big mortgage. Two of my children are in the school age, one is an apron-stringer. As for myself, I work with reasonable diligence; but as I am not so young as I once was, I know, deep within me, that I have slowed down a bit. I try to persuade myself that my personal ambitions and energies burn as brightly as they did. I know that they don't, for the simple reason that, more and more, I am shifting my hopes for achievement in the future to the slender shoulders of my youngsters. When a man gets in that frame of mind he is no longer young.

I am reciting all this just to identify myself. What I have said of myself reveals an average normal sort of situation. It is normal for a man of my age, in so far as the family and the slowing down of personal ambition are concerned. There are millions of other men in the same category. A wife, children, a small house and a big mortgage. I have to narrow my position, though. I work for a power company in a section where the Tennessee Valley Authority, as a Government agency, is a business competitor of my corporation employer.

> If the Tennessee Valley Authority is successful in the power business, the Government may also go into other business fields.

## Subsidized Competition

As a competitor, the Tennessee Valley Authority is paralleling my employer's lines [i.e., providing power along the same routes], underselling it because it is subsidized by the Government, and seeking, in every method, to destroy it. At this time, this area of

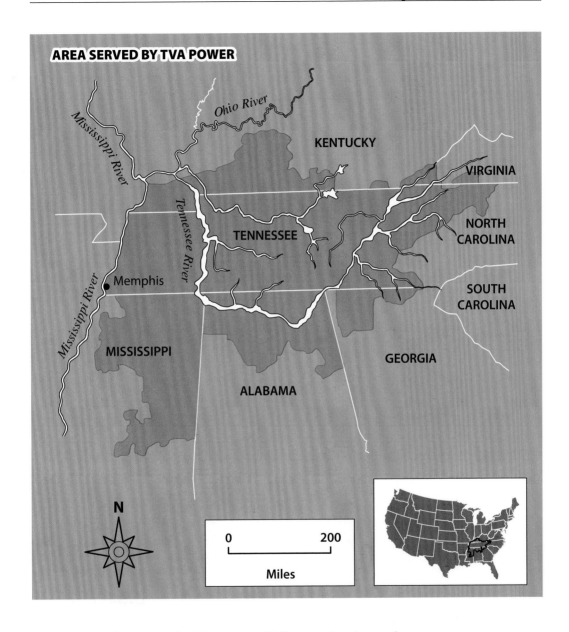

competition between the Tennessee Valley Authority and the power companies is limited to the states of Georgia, Tennessee, Alabama and a fringe of bordering states. If I understand this situation, among other objectives, this Tennessee Valley Authority is a Government "yardstick," and so is to measure the justness of rates which the

Government will ultimately charge. The Government plans a number of other concerns, similar to this first experiment, which will, at least in theory, serve much of the country and so, ultimately, eliminate many other privately owned power companies which employ a great many men. This is true, of course, only in the eventuality that the power companies are forced to the wall by Government-owned and supported organizations, which pay no taxes. The point is that my situation, which is not now so prevalent, bids fair to become more general.

If the Tennessee Valley Authority is successful in the power business, the Government may also go into other business fields. If I learn by watching straws in the wind, before very long there will be a great many other job holders with wives, children and a mortgage, whose employers will be faced with a destructive competition by the Government, to which I can see but one end. I cannot forecast that a privately owned business of any sort can compete for long against a hand which holds so tremendous a club. The Government can give unlimited financial backing to the untaxed Tennessee Valley Authority, or similar organization, and destroy the power companies, by stringent regulation and taxation, unless the courts intervene. Even courts may be "regulated." Being personal about it, unless there is a change in sentiment, my position—that is, of being about to lose my job at the hands of my own Government—in a few years will not be peculiar to me or to a section.

## Jobs on the Line

I am trying to keep from being egocentric or bitter. Every man thinks that his own troubles are the most important ones in the world, but when his troubles take on a general aspect he has the right to be heard. And then, there is so much written these days by the important men who are shaping Government policies in regard to the advantages of public power, there are so many loud-speaking politicians who air their views, that perhaps I, as one among many citizens for whom all these effusions are spread out for consumption, have the right to be heard. I certainly am vitally affected. I earn my daily bread from services which I give to this "Power Octopus" which the politicians rave against. I have troubles, but I am not talking about my own troubles alone, I'm offering myself as an example.

> " Under the guise of a larger mystical charity, our political leaders are going to put my employer out of business and take my job away from me. "

It's, of course, inappropriate for me to theorize extensively about the advantages or the disadvantages of the Tennessee Valley Authority and other organizations like it which are planned. Yet I can risk a few broad statements. They may be as good as anybody's.

Generally speaking, in the Tennessee Valley Authority experiment, the child was probably sired in all charitable sincerity. In the Tennessee Valley Authority official mouthpieces, there is still much talk about doing good for a section. Dams are to be built, soil erosion to be checked, the young encouraged to study folklore and what not. But, now that this Tennessee Valley Authority child is growing up, it appears to me that those soft words are used as a carefully planned system of camouflage. The Government is going into the power business. Before the importance of this Big Business, charity has only the permanency of a gentle dew—which may sound like a broad statement, needing support. In reality, it needs none. You don't have to support a machine gun in an argument against a cap pistol. I have respect for and fear of Big Business, very little for charity. In spite of loose talk, power, as an element of Big Business, is now the main issue, and today's Tennessee Valley Authority wouldn't know its first parents.

As for myself, I am an employee of a power company. I am not a stockholder, an executive or a director. The

Government, as I see it, announces on one hand that it has gone philanthropic, but through the agency of the Tennessee Valley Authority it is out after my employer's scalp and indirectly, out after my job and the jobs of a great many other people like me. Primarily, I am interested in my job and I hope that is being honest. . . . I thought it best, in so far as I see it, to dispose of the charitable side of the Tennessee Valley Authority in which I take no great store. Real charity is too difficult a job for any government.

## Asking Why the Government is Getting Involved

When I say that I am primarily interested in my job, and not in vague theories of future national welfare, a great many persons might feel it their duty to rise up and charge me with being selfish and unpatriotic. Well, I don't know about that. Charity begins at home, and so probably does patriotism. I'm not a Fourth of July orator. I'm a white-collar man, dependent on a job. This country is made up of men who are dependent upon smallish jobs to support their families. We are the ones for whom the important men theorize and make plans, and out of whose work come all the stock dividends and the taxes. . . .

My job and I stand between my family and the man who owns the mortgage on my house. My job and I stand between my family and the doctors, the grocerymen and the guys who sell me schoolbooks for my children and who, if I didn't stand where I did, would like to change the texts every year. I stand between this family of mine and the politicians, for the why I figure it out, under the guise of a larger mystical charity, our political leaders are going to put my employer out of business and take my job away from me. So far as I am concerned, my Government is taking sides with the crowd which tries to gobble up my pay check. So right at this point I stand

up and ask why. I ask why, because I'm one of the class of citizens for whose benefit it is said that all this whooping and hollering about uplift has been going on. It's true most of the talk about the advantages of the Tennessee Valley Authority has concerned a mystical national good, in a mystical future. I'm in the present, but my children are interested in the future. I speak for us both. I'm interested, but skeptical. Frankly speaking, I am about to lose my patriotism, such as it is.

When I raise that question "Why?" I open up a tremendous field for answers. A theorist could give me a book on the advantages of government ownership

President Franklin Roosevelt (far right), shown here at a TVA dam near Chattanooga, Tennessee, was more concerned about the country overall than he was about the job security of individual Americans. (**AP Images.**)

of power companies. I'm not interested in theories in books. I want to know what is the real reason that the Government is going to take away my job and put me and my family on relief, for I'm not young enough to get a new job, and I don't fool myself. I'm looking at this question from the stand-point of a man with a family and with a job, who is about to lose his livelihood at the hands of his own Government. I need an answer divorced from sentiment and vague charity. . . .

## A Political Move Benefiting Only Politicians

I answer my own question, and my answer is probably that of a good many others in like circumstances. I can't see it as a national emergency. The Tennessee Valley Authority and the whole attack on the Power Trust, Monopolies, or what have you, seem to me to be a political move, run essentially for the good of the politicians. For this statement I should probably be hanged. I make it nevertheless. Somebody has got to do a lot of explaining to convince me that my conclusion isn't true.

And why, then, do I feel that this Tennessee Valley Authority is political in purpose? And by that damning word "political" I mean it in its worst sense.

I don't think that politicians are anybody's fools, and when, early in the game, the leaders came out with the statement that the Tennessee Valley Authority was to be divorced from politics, I felt that nobody but an astute politician could have been that wise. Politicians know what the people think of them. The best way to use the organization ultimately and to profit from it was to deny knowing it.

> Politicians are not really interested in doing good for the people at large.

And then the immediate thought comes to me as to why they picked out the power industry to compete with, unless such competition had been carefully mapped out by the politically astute as a possible vote getter. I'll make the broad statement right here that politicians are not really interested in doing good for the people at large. Politicians are in a business, and that business is maintained by doing things which will get patronage for, and votes from, their constituents. At bedrock there is no sentiment in business or politics. As I see it, this attack on the power industry, as divorced from the minor uplift elements of the Tennessee Valley Authority, was worked out as being good issue to capture the popular imagination. When the people are restless at home, the way to cure that restlessness is to start a war of aggression. We were restless in the depression, so they started a war, and the power companies were the most logical victim for their purposes.

I work for a power company. Why didn't they start a war against the grocerymen or the druggists, for both of these essential industries are out to make money, just as my employer was and is? Well, the very words "Power Trust" were a sort of slogan and they could be used advantageously, for most people know very little about the power business. A politician could not well afford to rant against the grocery business, for there are too many grocery clerks, and the business is too well understood by the average man.

And do you think that the politicians didn't consider these things? That viewpoint would be really an insult to their intelligence.

## Starting a War for Political Profit

Of course, in this instance of the attack on the power companies, there may be small plausible excuses which border on public good. I'm not interested in small excuses, but I am in basic motives. We were in the depression and we needed a war to take our minds off our discontent. We had laws for the regulation and con-

> I have respect for my country, but I doubt the sincerity of the charitable politicians where their business interests are involved.

trol of industry, including the power industry. If we needed further laws to remedy abuses, those laws could have been passed. But regulation through orderly processes was not enough. We needed a war of aggression and destruction, not for the people's benefit, but for the benefit of the politicians who could point with pride at their achievements.

Does this sound unreasonably bitter? I doubt it. Ask the man with a job, after he has cooled down from the cheering at the political rally, what he thinks of the politicians. The politicians know the people's attitude themselves, for that is why they feel it is necessary to camouflage their purposes under this constant chatter about doing good.

And where do I come in? I'll answer that. I've got my job in which I have no capital, in the ordinary sense, but in which I have an investment of work and a certain amount of ability. Here is a war started against my job. I can see where soil erosion can be checked by a national program. I believe in flood control and reforestation. These are fields of activity which don't take away jobs, but which create them. But when they picked out the power industry for an apparently easy victory they went into a field which might have been controlled by due process of law, and sought to destroy the source of livelihood of a great many people, including mine.

Answers are so easy. The quick one here is that the Government, when it really gets down to the business of going into destructive competition with privately owned concerns, both in the power industry and outside of it, will make many charitable promises about taking care of old employees. Say, they call this the New Deal, don't they; or is it the New Game? War is war. For reasons of its own, the Government is centering all its programs toward helping the dissatisfied, the jobless and the young. There will be promises made to the old employees. They will promise bigger pay, as a sort of sentimental sop. It will be just a sop. The people who will be attracted by this new Governmental charity will constitute a mob. War is a destructive force and people, in a mob, enjoy pillage after a victory. A man who has worked for the "Power Octopus" would be as welcome around the new crowd as George Washington would be in a C.I.O. [Congress of Industrial Organizations] meeting.

I have respect for my country, but I doubt the sincerity of the charitable politicians where their business interests are involved. If my patriotism is to be aroused in this fight by the Government for the destruction of a well-established business which supports me—if that destruction is for the benefit of the jobless, the dissatisfied and the young—the politicians will have the hell of a time enlisting me on their side. I hope that it is clear. When the Government goes farther and farther into business of other sorts than power, you'll find a lot of other guys in my same frame of mind.

## Think of the Family Men

That's that! I've got one other thought to add. I believe in giving the boys and girls a chance, but you can't theorize the middle-aged men with families, wives and mortgages out of the picture. I remember, out of the past of my school days, that the Roman legion, in the days when Rome stood for something, was centered on one great principle. The strength of the legion was built around married men with families and property. The settled men, to use a common expression, were the ones who bore the brunt of the fighting when the young men fell back on them for protection. The idea was that the married men, who were fighting for their homes, wives and children would never run when the going got tough. It's just an idea, but it's worth thinking about when they run this country for the benefit and the experimenting of the jobless, the dissatisfied and the young.

And what will I do about it? How should I know? I'm just one among a very few, but our numbers will increase. To fall back on the illustrations of the Roman legion, I'm just one of the settled men who, normally, would hold the line intact when the experimental youngsters made unsuccessful reckless forays against the barbarians. I'm supposed to have property in my home and my job, and I'm supposed to be steady in a pinch. It's going to be the hell of a note when these youngsters and the jobless and the dissatisfied come back from their experimenting and look for the heavy-shouldered family men to withstand the attack which they provoked—and find that we're gone.

That eventually is worth thinking about—even worth the politicians thinking about.

# Lessons from the Depression Era Should Be Applied to the Current Economic Crisis

## Christina D. Romer

In the following viewpoint, Christina D. Romer, a professor of economics and a member of President Barack Obama's Council of Economic Advisers, draws parallels between the financial recovery measures enacted during the Great Depression and those measures that the current administration is employing to contend with the economic crisis that began in 2008. According to Romer, the administration should continue with its financial stimulus program—lending money to states and industries to keep Americans housed and employed—and keep this program going until the nation experiences real recovery. Romer also believes that monetary policy is important, as are policies that acknowledge the interdependence of global markets and their

**SOURCE.** Christina D. Romer, "Lessons from the Great Depression for Economic Recovery in 2009," Speech presented at the Brookings Institution, Washington, DC, March 9, 2009. Reproduced by permission.

importance in enabling widespread recovery. Romer maintains that the economic downturn will end and that the government must play a role in getting Americans to recognize that recovery will happen and thus ensure that investor and consumer confidence in the economy does not waver.

In the last few months [2009], I have found myself uttering the words "worst since the Great Depression" far too often: the worst twelve month job loss since the Great Depression; the worst financial crisis since the Great Depression; the worst rise in home foreclosures since the Great Depression. In my previous life, as an economic historian at [the University of California] Berkeley, one of the things I studied was the Great Depression. I thought it would be useful to reflect on that episode and what lessons it holds for policymakers today. In particular, what can we learn from the 1930s that will help us to end the worst recession since the Great Depression?

To start, let me point out that though the current recession is unquestionably severe, it pales in comparison with what our parents and grandparents experienced in the 1930s. Last Friday's [March 6, 2009] employment report showed that unemployment in the United States has reached 8.1%—a terrible number that signifies a devastating tragedy for millions of American families. But, at its worst, unemployment in the 1930s reached nearly 25%. And, that quarter of American workers had painfully few of the social safety nets that today help families maintain at least the essentials of life during unemployment. Likewise, following last month's revision of the GDP [gross domestic product] statistics, we know that real GDP has declined

> In the 1930s, the collapse of production and wealth led to bankruptcies and the disappearance of nearly half of American financial institutions.

almost 2% from its peak. But, between the peak in 1929 and the trough of the great Depression in 1933, real GDP fell over 25%.

I don't give these comparisons to minimize the pain the United States economy is experiencing today, but to provide some crucial perspective. Perhaps it is the historian and the daughter in me that finds it important to pay tribute to just what truly horrific conditions the previous generation of Americans endured and eventually triumphed over. And, it is the new policymaker in me that wants to be very clear that we are doing all that we can to make sure that the word "great" never applies to the current downturn.

While what we are experiencing is less severe than the Great Depression, there are parallels that make it a useful point of comparison and a source for learning about policy responses today. Most obviously, like the Great Depression, today's downturn had its fundamental cause in the decline in asset prices and the failure or near-failure of financial institutions. In 1929, the collapse and extreme volatility of stock prices led consumers and firms to simply stop spending. In the recent episode, the collapse of housing prices and stock prices has reduced wealth and shaken confidence, and led to sharp rises in the saving rate as consumers have hunkered down in the face of greatly reduced and much more uncertain wealth.

In the 1930s, the collapse of production and wealth led to bankruptcies and the disappearance of nearly half of American financial institutions. This, in turn, had two devastating consequences: a collapse of the money supply, as stressed by [economists] Milton Friedman and Anna Schwartz, and a collapse in lending, as stressed by [Federal Reserve chairman] Ben Bernanke. In the current episode, modern innovations such as derivatives led to a direct relationship between asset prices and severe stress in financial institutions. Over the fall [of 2008], we saw credit dry up and learned just how crucial lending is to the effective functioning of American businesses and households.

Another parallel is the worldwide nature of the decline. A key feature of the Great Depression was that virtually every industrial country experienced a severe contraction in production and a terrible rise in unemployment. This past year, there was hope that the current downturn might be mainly an American experience, and so world demand could remain high and perhaps help pull us through. However, during the past few months, we have realized that this hope was a false one. As statistics have poured in, we have learned that Europe, Asia, and many other areas are facing declines as large, if not larger, than our own. Indeed, rather than world demand helping to hold us up, the fall in U.S. demand has had a devastating impact on export economies such as Taiwan, China, and South Korea.

> The American Recovery and Reinvestment Act, passed less than thirty days after the Inauguration [of Barack Obama], is simply the biggest and boldest countercyclical fiscal action in history.

This similarity of causes between the Depression and today's recession means that President [Barack] Obama begins his presidency and his drive for recovery with many of the same challenges that Franklin Roosevelt faced in 1933. Our consumers and businesses are in no mood to spend or invest; our financial institutions are severely strained and hesitant to lend; short-term interest rates are effectively zero, leaving little room for conventional monetary policy; and world demand provides little hope for lifting the economy. Yet, the United States did recover from the Great Depression. What lessons can modern policymakers learn from that episode that could help them make the recovery faster and stronger today?

## Fiscal Stimulus Can Be Effective

One crucial lesson from the 1930s is that a small fiscal expansion has only small effects. I wrote a paper in 1992 that said that fiscal policy was not the key engine of recovery in the Depression. From this, some have concluded that I do not believe fiscal policy can work today or could have worked in the 1930s. Nothing could be farther than the truth. My argument paralleled [professor of economics] E. Cary Brown's famous conclusion that in the Great Depression, fiscal policy failed to generate recovery "not because it does not work, but because it was not tried."

The key fact is that while Roosevelt's fiscal actions were a bold break from the past, they were nevertheless small relative to the size of the problem. When Roosevelt took office in 1933, real GDP was more than 30% below its normal trend level. (For comparison, the U.S. economy is currently estimated to be between 5 and 10% below trend.) The emergency spending that Roosevelt did was precedent-breaking—balanced budgets had certainly been the norm up to that point. But, it was quite small. The deficit rose by about one and a half percent of GDP in 1934. One reason the rise wasn't larger was that a large tax increase had been passed at the end of the [Herbert] Hoover administration. Another key fact is that fiscal expansion was not sustained. The deficit declined in fiscal 1935 by roughly the same amount that it had risen in 1934. Roosevelt also experienced the same inherently procyclical behavior of state and local fiscal actions that President Obama is facing. Because of balanced budget requirements, state and local governments are forced to cut spending and raise tax rates when economic activity declines and state tax revenues fall. At the same time that Roosevelt was running unprecedented federal deficits, state and local governments were switching to running surpluses to get their fiscal houses in order. The result was that the total fiscal expansion in the 1930s was very small indeed. As a result, it could only have a modest direct impact on the state of the economy.

This is a lesson the Administration has taken to heart. The American Recovery and Reinvestment Act, passed less than thirty days after the Inauguration, is simply the biggest and boldest countercyclical fiscal action in history. The nearly $800 billion fiscal stimulus is roughly equally divided between tax cuts, direct government investment spending, and aid to the states and people directly hurt by the recession. The fiscal stimulus is close to 3% of GDP in each of the next two years. And, as I mentioned, a good chunk of this stimulus takes the form of fiscal relief to state governments, so that they do not have to balance their budgets only by such measures as raising taxes and cutting the employment of nurses, teachers, and first responders. We expect this fiscal expansion to be extremely important to countering the terrible job loss that last Friday's [March 6, 2009] numbers show now totals 4.4 million since the recession began fourteen months ago [in January 2008].

While the direct effects of fiscal stimulus were small in the Great Depression, I think it is important to acknowledge that there may have been an indirect effect. Roosevelt's very act of doing something must have come as a great relief to a country that had been suffering depression for more than three years. To have a President step up to the challenge and say the country would attack the Depression with the same fervor and strength it would an invading army surely lessened uncertainty and calmed fears. Also, signature programs such as the WPA [Works Progress Administration] that directly hired millions of workers no doubt contributed to a sense of progress and control. In this way, Roosevelt's actions may have been more beneficial than the usual estimates of fiscal policy suggest. If the actions President Obama is taking in the current downturn can generate the same kind of confidence effects, they may also be more effective than estimates based on conventional multipliers would lead one to believe.

## Increase the Money Supply

A second key lesson from the 1930s is that monetary expansion can help to heal an economy even when interest rates are near zero. In the same paper where I said fiscal policy was not key in the recovery from the Great Depression, I argued that monetary expansion was very useful. But, the monetary expansion took a surprising form [during the Depression]: it was essentially a policy of quantitative easing conducted by the U.S. Treasury.

The United States was on a gold standard throughout the Depression. Part of the explanation for why the Federal Reserve did so little to counter the financial panics and economic decline was that it was fighting to defend the gold standard and maintain the prevailing fixed exchange rate. In April 1933, Roosevelt temporarily suspended the convertibility to gold and let the dollar depreciate substantially. When we went back on gold at the new higher price, large quantities of gold flowed into the U.S. Treasury from abroad. These gold inflows serendipitously continued throughout the mid-1930s, as political tensions mounted in Europe and investors sought the safety of U.S. assets.

Under a gold standard, the Treasury could increase the money supply without going through the Federal Reserve. It was allowed to issue gold certificates, which were interchangeable with Federal Reserve notes, on the basis of the gold it held. When gold flowed in, the Treasury issued more notes. The result was that the money supply, defined narrowly as currency and reserves, grew by nearly 17% per year between 1933 and 1936.

This monetary expansion couldn't lower nominal interest rates[1] because they were already near zero. What it could do was break expectations of deflation. Prices had fallen 25% between 1929 and 1933. People through-

Like Franklin Roosevelt in the Depression, U.S. President Barack Obama took office amid a financial crisis that demanded federal intervention. (Pete Souza/White House via Getty Images.)

out the economy expected this deflation to continue. As a result, the real cost of borrowing and investing was exceedingly high. Consumers and businesses wanted to sit on any cash they had because they expected its real purchasing power to increase as prices fell. Devaluation followed by rapid monetary expansion broke this deflationary spiral. Expectations of rapid deflation were replaced by expectations of price stability or even some inflation. This change in expectations brought real interest rates[2] down dramatically.

The change in the real cost of borrowing and investing appears to have had a beneficial impact on consumer and firm behavior. The first thing that turned around was interest-sensitive spending. For example, car sales surged in the summer of 1933. One sign that lower real interest rates were crucial is that real fixed investment and consumer spending on durables both rose dramatically between 1933 and 1934, while consumer spending on services barely budged.

In thinking about the lessons from the Great Depression for today, I want to tread very carefully. A key rule of my current job [as part of President Obama's Council of Economic Advisers] is that I do not comment on Federal Reserve policy. So, let me be very clear—I am not advocating going on a gold standard just so we can go off it again, or that [U.S. secretary of the treasury] Tim Geithner should start conducting rogue monetary policy. But the experience of the 1930s does suggest that monetary policy can continue to have an important role to play even when interest rates are low by affecting expectations, and in particular, by preventing expectations of deflation.

> " The experience of the 1930s does suggest that monetary policy can continue to have an important role to play even when interest rates are low by affecting expectations, and in particular, by preventing expectations of deflation. "

## Keep the Stimulus Going

This discussion of fiscal and monetary policy in the 1930s leads me to a third lesson from the Great Depression: beware of cutting back on stimulus too soon.

As I have just described, monetary policy was very expansionary in the mid-1930s. Fiscal policy, though less expansionary, was also helpful. Indeed, in 1936 it was inadvertently stimulatory. Largely because of political pressures, Congress overrode Roosevelt's veto and gave World War I veterans a large bonus. This caused another one-time rise in the deficit of more than 1½% of GDP.

And, the economy responded. Growth was very rapid in the mid-1930s. Real GDP increased 11% in 1934, 9% in 1935, and 13% in 1936. Because the economy was beginning at such a low level, even these growth rates were not enough to bring it all the way back to normal. Industrial production finally surpassed its July 1929 peak in December 1936, but was still well below the level predicted by the pre-Depression trend. Unemployment had fallen by close to 10 percentage points—but was still over 15%. The economy was on the road to recovery, but still precarious and not yet at a point where private demand was ready to carry the full load of generating growth.

In this fragile environment, fiscal policy turned sharply contractionary. The one-time veterans' bonus ended, and Social Security taxes were collected for the first time in 1937. As a result, the deficit was reduced by roughly 2½% of GDP.

Monetary policy also turned inadvertently contractionary. The Federal Reserve was becoming increasingly concerned about inflation in 1936. It was also concerned that, because banks were holding such large quantities of excess reserves, open-market operations would merely cause banks to substitute government bonds for excess reserves and would have no impact on lending. In an effort to put themselves in a position where they could tighten if they needed to, the Federal Reserve doubled reserve requirements in three steps in 1936 and 1937. Unfortunately, banks, shaken by the bank runs of just a few years before, scrambled to build reserves above the new higher required levels. As a result, interest rates rose and lending plummeted.

The results of the fiscal and monetary double whammy in the precarious environment were disastrous. GDP rose by only 5% in 1937 and then fell by 3% in 1938, and unemployment rose dramatically, reaching 19% in 1938. Policymakers soon reversed course and the strong recovery resumed, but taking the wrong turn in 1937 effectively added two years to the Depression.

The 1937 episode is an important cautionary tale for modern policymakers. At some point, recovery will take on a life of its own, as rising output generates rising investment and inventory demand through accelerator effects, and confidence and optimism replace caution and pessimism. But, we will need to monitor the economy closely to be sure that the private sector is back in the saddle before government takes away its crucial lifeline.

## Set Short- and Long-Term Goals

The fourth lesson we can draw from the recovery of the 1930s is that financial recovery and real recovery go together. When Roosevelt took office, his immediate actions were largely focused on stabilizing a collapsing financial system. He declared a national Bank Holiday two days after his inauguration, effectively shutting every bank in the country for a week while the books were checked. This 1930s version of a "stress test" led to the permanent closure of more than 10% of the nation's banks, but improved confidence in the ones that remained. As I discussed before, Roosevelt temporarily suspended the gold standard, before going back on gold at a lower value for the dollar, paving the way for increases in the money supply. In June 1933, Congress passed legislation establishing deposit insurance through the FDIC [Federal Deposit Insurance Corporation] and helping homeowners through the Home Owners Loan Corporation. The actual rehabilitation of financial institutions obviously took much longer. Indeed, much of the hard work of recapitalizing banks and dealing with distressed homeowners and farmers was spread out over 1934 and 1935.

Nevertheless, the immediate actions to stabilize the financial system had dramatic short-run effects on financial markets. Real stock prices rose over 40% from March to May 1933, commodity prices soared, and interest-rate spreads shrank. And, the actions surely contributed to the economy's rapid growth after 1933, as wealth rose,

> "When Roosevelt took office, his immediate actions were largely focused on stabilizing a collapsing financial system. . . . The actual rehabilitation of financial institutions obviously took much longer."

confidence improved, and bank failures and home fore-closures declined.

But, it was only after the real recovery was well established that the financial recovery took firm hold. Real stock prices in March 1935 were more than 10% lower than in May 1933; bank lending continued falling until mid-1935; and real house prices rose only 7% from 1933 to 1935. The strengthening real economy improved the health of the financial system. Bank profits moved from large and negative in 1933 to large and positive in 1935, and remained high through the end of the Depression, with the result that bank suspensions were minimal after 1933. Real stock prices rose robustly. Business failures and home foreclosures fell sharply and almost without interruption after 1932. And, this virtuous cycle continued as the financial recovery led to further narrowing of interest-rate spreads and increased willingness of banks to lend.

This lesson is another one that has been prominent in the minds of policymakers today. The [Obama] Administration has from the beginning sought to create a comprehensive recovery program. The Financial Stabilization Plan, which involves evaluating the capital needs of financial institutions, as well as crucial programs to directly increase lending, is central to putting the financial system back to work for American industry and households. Together with the Administration's housing plan, these financial rescue measures should provide the lending and stability needed for economic growth. The fiscal stimulus package was designed to create jobs quickly. In doing so, it should lower defaults and improve balance sheets so that our financial system can continue to strengthen.

## Think and Act with a Global Perspective

The fifth lesson from the Great Depression is that worldwide expansionary policy shares the burdens and the benefits of recovery. Research by [economists] Barry Eichengreen and Jeffrey Sachs shows that going off the gold standard and increasing the domestic money supply was a key factor in generating recovery and growth across a wide range of countries in the 1930s. Importantly, these actions worked to lower world interest rates and benefit other countries, rather than to just shift expansion from one country to another.

> The more that countries throughout the world can move toward monetary and fiscal expansion, the better off we all will be.

The implications for today are obvious. The more that countries throughout the world can move toward monetary and fiscal expansion, the better off we all will be. In this regard, the aggressive fiscal action in China and the reduction in interest rates in Europe and the U.K. announced last week were welcome news. They are paving the way for a worldwide end to this worldwide recession.

## Know That Recovery Will Happen

The final lesson that I want to draw from the 1930s is perhaps the most crucial. A key feature of the Great Depression is that it did eventually end. Despite the devastating loss of wealth, chaos in our financial markets, and a loss of confidence so great that it nearly destroyed Americans' fundamental faith in capitalism, the economy came back. Indeed, the growth between 1933 and 1937 was the highest we have ever experienced outside of wartime. Had the U.S. not had the terrible policy-induced setback in 1937, we, like most other countries in the world, would probably have been fully recovered before the outbreak of World War II.

This fact should give Americans hope. We are starting from a position far stronger than our parents and grandparents were in in 1933. And, the policy response has been fast, bold, and well-conceived. If we continue to heed the lessons of the Great Depression, there is every reason to believe that we will weather this trial and come through to the other side even stronger than before.

## Notes

1. Nominal interest rates are the stated interest to be paid on a loan; they may not reflect the true rate, or actual cost, to the borrower.
2. Real interest rates reflect an adjustment for expected inflation and indicate the real cost to the borrower.

# International Depression Conditions Today Are Similar to Those in the 1930s

## Bruce Campbell

In the viewpoint that follows, Bruce Campbell contends that the global financial crisis that began in 2008 bears some similarity to the Great Depression. In Campbell's view, both disasters began with economic collapse in the United States, as unregulated markets and Wall Street stratagems promoted the accumulation of too much unsecured debt. Campbell is optimistic, though, that speedy global governmental response to the contemporary crisis—including the implementation of huge stimulus packages—may correct the downturn before global economies reach the depths experienced in the 1930s. Bruce Campbell is the director of the Canadian Centre for Policy

SOURCE. Bruce Campbell, "The Global Economic Crisis and Its Canadian Dimension: Economic Downturn Is Already as Bad as in the Early 1930s," *CCPA Monitor*, vol. 16, July 1, 2009, pp. 30–34. Reproduced by permission of Canadian Centre for Policy Alternatives. www.policyalternatives.ca.

Alternatives, an independent research institute that focuses on social and economic justice.

There is still an air of disbelief in Canada about the severity of the current [2009] global recession—now widely accepted as the worst since the Great Depression of the 1930s—both as it is affecting Canada and as it is playing out around the world.

Perhaps it is because recession came later to Canada and is just beginning to hit hard. Or maybe it is because government leaders and media keep assuring Canadians that we are in good shape to weather the storm and the worst will be over "soon."

> Leading global indicators in these early days are as bad or worse than they were in the first stages of the Great Depression of the 1930s.

To be sure, for the hundreds of thousands of Canadians who have already lost their jobs and the many more who feel threatened, the reality of recession is hitting home. Manufacturing communities like Windsor and scores of forestry communities have been devastated.

But for many, at least at this early stage, the signs are subtle. There is a veneer of normalcy. Most people may still be several degrees of separation from direct experience of friends and acquaintances who are losing their jobs, losing their homes, declaring bankruptcy, seeing their retirement savings shrink. The recession is still to a surprising extent a business page story in the newspapers.

We in Canada seem far from the public outrage and popular mobilization that is occurring in Europe and elsewhere—but perhaps that's because the media spotlight has not yet focused on plant occupations, demonstrations, and other manifestations of public discontent. . . .

## Grim Indicators of Global Crisis

Leading global indicators in these early days are as bad or worse than they were in the first stages of the Great Depression of the 1930s. The world's industrial output is contracting as sharply as it did in 1929. International trade volumes are falling much faster than they did in 1929. According to the United Nations, world trade declined at an annual rate of more than 40% in the first quarter of 2009.

The OECD [Organization for Economic Co-Operation and Development] predicts that the global economy will shrink by 2.75% in 2009, its worst performance since the Great Depression. Advanced industrialized country economies are predicted to shrink by 4.3%. The OECD and other international forecasting agencies have been revising their forecasts downwards for the last six months.

Risk-laden financial instruments devised at the J.P. Morgan Chase investment bank helped fuel the 2008 market crash. (**Chris Hondros/Getty Images.**)

The IMF [International Monetary Fund] is pointing to "worrisome parallels" between the current crisis and the 1930s. It warns that, unless corrective action is taken, "the human consequences could be absolutely devastating." The International Labour Organization (ILO) predicts that the jobless numbers globally will rise by 38 million (20%) in 2009, reaching 231 million.

The UN [United Nations] commission of experts on international financial and monetary reform warned that 200 million people, mostly in developing countries, could be pushed into deep poverty unless action is taken to confront the effects of the crisis. . . .

## Factors Responsible for the Crash

As in 1929, this economic crisis was precipitated by a U.S. financial crisis. Unlike 1929, the crisis followed a worldwide financial boom reflected in the explosion of foreign holdings of U.S. asset-backed securities. The global value of financial assets had grown to $160 trillion by September 2008—three and a half times larger than the value of global GDP [gross domestic product].

The crisis spread very rapidly from the U.S. epicentre due to the highly integrated nature of financial markets, causing a rare synchronized global economic recession. And the financial crisis and the real economy recession have been interacting in a mutually reinforcing way. . . .

> Far from reducing risk, securitized mortgage derivatives increased risk and made the financial system more prone to crisis.

This boom was overseen by Alan Greenspan, chairman of the U.S. Federal Reserve, who believed that markets knew best how to evaluate and manage risk without the heavy hand of regulation. Greenspan kept interest rates low and allowed a housing bubble and a stock bubble to develop. He supported unregulated subprime mortgage lending and derivatives.

The biggest culprit, however, was Wall Street, which, with its enormous political influence, successfully lobbied for financial deregulation and created the financial instruments and their complex—supposedly risk-reducing—mathematical models that drove the boom to dizzying heights.

Two key financial innovations were at the heart of the crash. The first, securitized mortgage derivatives (also called collateralized debt obligations, or CDOs), were invented by a team at investment bank J.P. Morgan in the late 1990s. Individual mortgage loans were pooled and packaged into new cash-flow-producing assets—mortgage-backed securities—and then sold to investors. They were presented as instruments that would spread and thereby reduce risk, and bank regulators were persuaded to lower the threshold of capital reserves that banks were required to hold against default on these derivatives, compared to traditional loan requirements.

Securitization severed the traditional direct link between lender and borrower. Purchasers of these bundled mortgages had no idea of their quality. As business boomed, credit derivatives were extended to sub-prime mortgages, put into what Nobel Prize–winning economist Paul Krugman called "the financial juicer," and came out the other end guaranteed AAA by deeply conflicted credit rating agencies whose incomes were paid by the very institutions whose financial products they were evaluating.

They offered higher returns than Treasury bills and other conventional securities. The promise—that this would make the financial system stronger by spreading risk widely—was a lie. Far from reducing risk, securitized mortgage derivatives increased risk and made the financial system more prone to crisis.

Securitized mortgage derivatives were sliced into portions that were assigned a hierarchy of different risk levels and different rates of return. Investors could

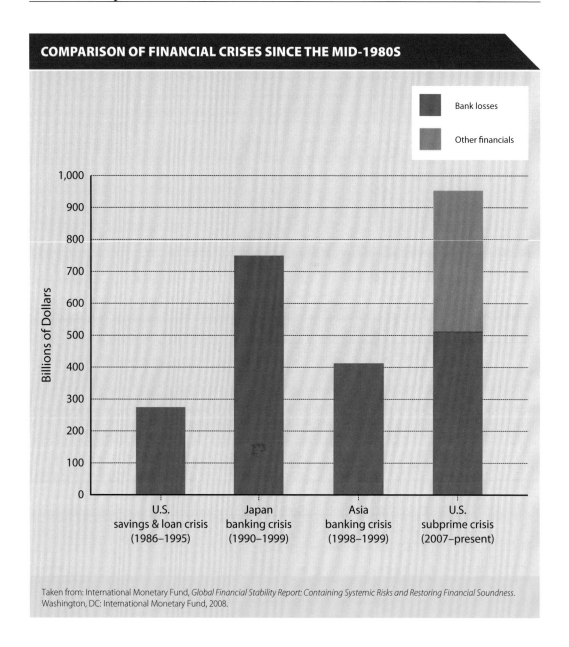

**COMPARISON OF FINANCIAL CRISES SINCE THE MID-1980S**

Bank losses

Other financials

Billions of Dollars

U.S.
savings & loan crisis
(1986–1995)

Japan
banking crisis
(1990–1999)

Asia
banking crisis
(1998–1999)

U.S.
subprime crisis
(2007–present)

Taken from: International Monetary Fund, *Global Financial Stability Report: Containing Systemic Risks and Restoring Financial Soundness.* Washington, DC: International Monetary Fund, 2008.

choose their preferred level of risk within the bundle. From the original derivative, others firms created a complicated pyramid of secondary derivatives, repackaging its high-risk slices and selling them to unwitting investors as low-risk slices. . . .

The notional outstanding value of credit derivatives (including mortgages and other debt, from car loans to credit card debt) had, by the end of 2007, reached a mind-boggling $596 *trillion*, almost four times the value of all global financial assets, and more than 10 times the value of world GDP.

## Phony Insurance Contracts

The other financial villain was credit default swaps (CDSs). These insurance-like contracts—also invented by J.P. Morgan—were used by investors to hedge against default on their mortgage-backed derivatives. Buyers of credit default swaps could then move these assets, and the accompanying risk, off their books. Compared to the (now) lower capital requirements for the original mortgage derivatives, CDS sellers like insurance giant AIG were required to post even less capital reserves against default. Secretive and largely exempt from regulation, these phony insurance contracts—which [businessman and financier] Warren Buffet called "financial weapons of mass destruction"—greatly magnified the credit derivative bubble. By the end of 2007, the CDS market had reached $62 trillion, larger than the world's total GDP.

> In the wake of the September 2008 financial crash, the [International Monetary Fund] now estimates that there are $4.4 trillion worth of toxic assets (bad debt) held by investors in the U.S. and around the world.

As U.S. housing prices continued their slide and the magnitude of sub-prime mortgage defaults became known in mid-2007, those who had sold CDS insurance to investors holding now worthless mortgage credit derivatives could no longer meet their obligations to compensate these investors, and either went bankrupt, like Lehman Brothers, or were bailed out by the government, like Bank of America, Citicorp, and AIG.

In the wake of the September 2008 financial crash, the IMF now estimates that there are $4.4 trillion worth of toxic assets (bad debt) held by investors in the U.S. and around the world. And the figure will undoubtedly grow as more toxic debt is uncovered. . . .

## International Response to the Crisis

On the positive side, governments do not seem to be repeating the worst mistakes of their 1929 counterparts. In response to the crisis, interest rates are being cut more rapidly and from a lower level. Central bankers are rapidly expanding the money supply, unlike their Great Depression predecessors who cut the money supply early, with catastrophic economic consequences. And governments today are much more willing than their 1930s counterparts to run fiscal deficits, though stimulus spending to date falls far short of what is required.

The G-20[1] leaders met in London last April [2009] to take the first formally coordinated steps in confronting the crisis. There are major differences in how participating nations perceive the nature and severity of the crisis, as well as the necessary solutions. The United States, China, and Japan are the leading proponents of boosting aggregate demand through aggressive fiscal stimulus. Germany and France are leading the group of European Union countries that think the main focus should be financial stabilization, reform, and re-regulation.

> The biggest shortcoming of the G-20 [an economic collective] is the inadequacy of the fiscal stimulus response to the collapse of global demand.

The final G-20 communiqué begins the process of creating a new regulatory architecture for global finance, including regulatory frameworks for hedge funds and credit-rating agencies, a framework for CEO pay, greater transparency from tax havens, and commitments from governments to backstop their banks with capital, if necessary.

It also commits to an injection of short-term trade finance, as well as a major increase in resources for the IMF, including funding for a new issue of Special Drawing Rights (SDRs) [government and central bank holdings used to stabilize international exchange rates]. How effective this will be in meeting the severe economic and financial challenges facing emerging and developing economies will depend on the degree of conditionality associated with this finance. Whether the IMF will depart from its traditional demands—for public spending cuts and other anti-stimulus measures—remains to be seen, though recent loans to Ukraine, Latvia, and Pakistan are not encouraging.

## Potential Inadequacies

Although the G-20 communiqué makes important commitments, these commitments are not only voluntary, but they also fall short of what is needed. Many are vague, and there are no collective enforcement measures. It remains to be seen whether nations will live up to their pledges. More fundamentally, it casts doubt on whether the current system will be sufficiently transformed to prevent future crises.

The biggest shortcoming of the G-20 is the inadequacy of the fiscal stimulus response to the collapse of global demand. Most major industrialized countries, including Canada, have fallen short of the IMF target. As economist Robert Schiller points out, "The greatest risk is that appropriate stimulus will be derailed by doubters who still do not appreciate the true condition of our economy."

The G-20 communiqué takes a strong stand against trade protectionism, but ignores the threat of protectionist measures that could occur as a reaction to nations that do not pull their weight on the fiscal stimulus front and are seen to be free-riding off nations that do. An important lesson of the Great Depression is not that protectionism made things worse (which it did), but rather that it was the macroeconomic policy failures that created the conditions that made protectionism inevitable. Protectionism, like currency wars, was a second-order effect. Under these circumstances, protectionism was a rational reaction; and it took a long time to reverse.

## Note

1. Refers to the Group of Twenty Finance Ministers and Central Bank Governors—an economic collective from developed nations.

# CHAPTER 3

# Personal Narratives

# Ingenuity and Faith Help a Family Through Hard Times

## Mrs. Duncan Pearmain

Many stories of the Great Depression portray the hardship that the economic downturn forced on U.S. citizens. Mrs. Duncan Pearmain had a somewhat different experience during the latter years of the decade. Writing the following viewpoint in 1939, she recounts her family's decision to move from the East Coast to California and open a boarding house. While the decision was spurred by many of the same economic woes that plagued her neighbors, Pearmain remained confident in her ability to achieve success through hard work. She explains how she and her husband were able to purchase a boarding house with no down payment, acquire the needed household furnishings through credit and the trust of others, and turn a small initial investment into the ownership of multiple apartment homes. Pearmain argues that this type of determination and ingenuity—not government

**SOURCE.** Mrs. Duncan Pearmain, "Salute the Thirty-Niners!" *Saturday Evening Post*, vol. 211, May 13, 1939, pp. 18, 51–54. Copyright © 1939 Saturday Evening Post Society. Reproduced by permission.

intervention—will pull the country out of the depression. Mrs. Duncan Pearmain's narrative appeared in the *Saturday Evening Post*, a periodical that was founded in 1728 and remains in print today.

Many stories of struggle and success have glorified the pioneers of yesterday—the now-famous Forty-niners [referring to the individuals who flocked to California in search of gold beginning in 1848]—and I burn to tell the story of today's pioneers, the Thirty-niners, for I am one of them.

The Thirty-niners are conquering today's frontier—that frontier which spreads over all America and which we have called "Depression." We are, like all pioneers, willing to meet the exigencies of our time, no matter what toil, so long as independence and hope of an independent future are sustained. We want our children to be free of fear, want them to know a better world than this alphabet one[1] we now live in.

## The Importance of Family

One of the things the depression pioneers have learned is that teamwork is invaluable, that marriage means being partners. Women like being partners. We find it tiring, though not tiresome. But it is hard on the men, for theirs is the job of guaranteeing the daily needs, often watching their wives working at the thing they would like to be doing.

So it is with Duncan and me. His job guarantees today; my job may guarantee tomorrow.

We went into our venture for the same reason that motivated the other pioneers. Duncan was not making enough for us to live and make progress. And progress means putting something aside, having an investment that gives one hope that the future will be secure. And, too, there is the glory of the fight. Win, lose or draw, there is the beautiful welding of purpose that two people in love find enduring and fine.

We once had security—or thought we did—and then we did not have it. That made us Twenty-niners.

The question was how to rebuild? After all the debts were paid we had $282.02. Don't overlook the two cents; a good banker wouldn't. It was up to Duncan to start from scratch, which he did. Our family consisted of grandpa, grandma, our small daughter, Pat, Duncan and me. We carried on, getting no place, just treading water.

> The price of rent in decent Eastern neighborhoods was high. We could think of only one thing—to get free rent, and the only way we knew to get free rent was to own an apartment house.

## The Decision to Move to California

In the fall of '36 Duncan landed a traveling job that seemed like riches, for it paid $126 every two weeks. The new job kept Duncan away from home four to six months at a time. His car expenses were paid, but he had to pay his hotel and food bills. We were not so rich after all. Grandpa died—that left us sick at heart and took all the savings. Grandma needed a change—sunshine and warmth.

When Duncan came home for grandpa's funeral, we fell into the old discussion of how to get ahead, how to save. The price of rent in decent Eastern neighborhoods was high. We could think of only one thing—to get free rent, and the only way we knew to get free rent was to own an apartment house.

We came to our decision during his visit home—that we'd move to California. Dunc's territory consisted of all the states west of the Mississippi, and we felt that for us to live in New York would mean we would never have Dunc with us. He went back to his job, and grandma and I disposed of the household goods. It was the last week in November, 1936, before we got started in our small car on the westward trek.

## Finding the Perfect House

By the time we arrived in California, ten days before Christmas, 1936, I was raring to go.

We took a small apartment and I set out to learn something about the real-estate situation. I found one could get a temporary six-months' real-estate license in this fair state for the sum of three dollars and the sponsoring of a reliable agent. I found such an agent our second day in California, a big booming man who chuckled at my idea of buying an apartment with nothing down, but who seemed to get a kick out of helping me.

I explained quite frankly that my idea in having a license was so that whatever broker I bought from would have to give me half the commission when we paid our necessary payments to the former owner.

On the sixth day, the agent said, "To buy a place on the terms you offer, you'd have to find an owner who was most anxious to be rid of something."

On the seventh day he showed me a place in a very fine suburban neighborhood. It had the one qualification about which I was adamant—it was near the ocean, with a superb view of water and mountains. The suburb had been rezoned and an apartment house of eight units was the only one that would ever be in that particular section of the suburb. It was in the midst of homes costing fifteen thousand and upward, and it had a very unkempt look beside the beautifully groomed houses and lawns of its neighbors.

The lots adjacent to the building were vacant. I was to learn that the neighbors considered the place an eyesore and wished it would burn down. I was also to learn that the place had never rented well, and that several of the tenants were relatives of the owner. The owner lived in Arizona and the place had a resident manager, we understood.

I was wild with excitement. I wired Dunc:

FOUND PERFECT PLACE. BEAUTIFUL NEIGH-
BORHOOD. ORIGINALLY COST $24,000. CAN BE
BOUGHT FOR $10,500. COMPLETELY FURNISHED.
EIGHT APARTMENTS. AGENT THINKS TERMS
CAN BE ARRANGED, OWNER LIVES IN ARIZONA.
COME AND BUY IT. LOVE.

Dunc arrived the day after Christmas, via share-expense auto—a cheap way of traveling. Before going to meet him I hocked my wedding ring, so that we could eat and buy gasoline that week. In the excitement Dunc never noticed my ringless hand, for which I was grateful.

## A Good Deal on the House

When he saw the beautiful location and the big off-color-white stucco building, he glowed with enthusiasm. He girded his loins and went into battle and put up some fighting arguments of which I shall always be proud. The owner came up from Arizona and the battle raged for several days. Dunc scared me by declaring the place wasn't worth a dime more than $9000. When he said that, I kicked him so viciously on the shin that it raised a welt. I thought he'd spoil everything by going Scotch on me. The owner came down to $9500. I was dumfounded.

Having won that point, Dunc then proceeded to argue terms. An accepted method of buying was this—the buyer would pay at least 20 per cent of the purchase price down and then 1 per cent per month thereafter, for a specified number of years, at the end of which time the buyer had to refinance.

> We had bought an apartment without a penny.

Duncan argued that we would make high monthly payments that would, in twelve months, equal a 20 per cent down payment plus the 1 per cent per month payments. It worked like this: We would pay $250 per month for the first twelve months and thereafter the usual 1 per cent, or $95. The owner would, therefore, at the end of twelve months, have received $3000—exactly forty dollars less than he would receive by the regular procedure. And on this basis we bought the place.

After Dunc and the seller came to this agreement there was still the expense of escrow, title searching, and so on. Duncan argued that the seller must pay all such expenses, and a day went to that.

We had bought an apartment without a penny. Duncan had to leave via share-expense auto at ten o'clock the second day of January, and when he left we had seventy-three cents between us.

Now, his salary was $252 per month. Therefore, it took all but two dollars of that for the first payment to the bank which was to act as collection agent. His first-of-the-month check would be in Omaha, waiting for him when he arrived there, and he would get another on the fifteenth. Of this, Dunc was to send me $200; he said he was willing to go without anything, on the chance to get ahead, and he could stay in Y.M.C.A.'s and would not spend more than forty cents per day for food. This he has done for two years. He could get along on his $52 a month easily, he declared. He has done on much less many and many a month. When our few household goods arrived, I was to sell or hock some of the old family silver for us to live on and to make up the extra fifty which he couldn't send.

## Unforeseen Problems

The money arrived from Duncan promptly, and I planked it down with great pride. On the twenty-fifth, the manager for the absentee owner was to leave, at which time she was to give us an itemized accounting of every spoon and piece of furniture in the place and we would take her apartment. Everything looked rosy, for wouldn't the rents start rolling in on the first?

But it didn't work that way. On the twenty-fifth the manager left, and as she was leaving she handed me the inventory sheets. She drove off. Gram and I went into her vacant apartment. It was bare! She left behind one table and two straight-backed chairs. On checking, I found she was entirely within her rights; the furniture belonged to her. But there we were, without a mattress to sleep upon. She had even taken the stoves.

Gram and I were thunderstruck. We sat on the two straight-backed chairs in the cold room and went over the inventory sheets. There was little on them, and that little, we were to find, was too shabby to offer to a discriminating public. We were devastated.

"The wolf's sure at the door this time!" gram said.

My daughter, Pat, sitting on the floor, started laughing and kidding me. "So we own an apartment house now? Some dump!"

I left the place, got in my trusty car and drove to the ocean front. After some time I decided there was nothing I could do but find someone who would trust me. I drove up and down the streets of the nearest small city and located a big secondhand place with some good-looking stuff out on the sidewalk. The owner was a Jew and a gentleman. I told him my story—the exact, painful truth.

Mr. Levi listened carefully, nodding and smiling sometimes. "And you ain't got a drop of Jewish blood in you?" he joked.

"Not a drop. But I've got pioneer blood. My great-grandmother landed in a strange country with a cherry-wood bedstead and some rosebushes."

He laughed. "I trust you. You come now and pick what you want."

# The Trust of a Stranger

I almost kissed his whiskered old face. I went in debt for a good stove, coil springs, inner-spring mattresses—secondhand, sterilized—an easy chair for gram, and then I saw a rug I liked. It was priced at thirty-five dollars.

"When gram saw the truckload of bare necessities, she smiled on me in a way that still brings tears to my eyes.

Mr. Levi saw me looking at it, and said, "Sure, you take it too. When I trust somebody, I trust 'em."

Bare floors are cold for gram, even in California. I took it. I took a chest of drawers, a kitchen table and chairs, a gas heater.

It was 5:30 when we pulled up at our newly acquired property, later to be called by the family "Acquisition 1." Mr. Levi and his helper in the truck were behind me. Gram and Pat were desolate, hungry. When gram saw the truckload of bare necessities, she smiled on me in a way that still brings tears to my eyes.

The coil springs were laid on the bedroom floor, the mattresses on the springs, the rug laid in the living room, the easy chair placed before the gas heater, and then Mr. Levi and his helper attached the heater and the kitchen stove. How cozy, how good it felt.

As we dined on canned beans, spinach and bread, Pat said, "Well, the wolf wasn't at the door, after all."

"Oh, yes, he was," grandma nodded emphatically. "But your mamma went to the door to meet him and came back with a fur coat." This sent Pat into gales of laughter. "It's the truth," gram nodded emphatically. "It's just like my days in Minnesota. Only it was a coyote, and I shot him and skinned him."

"Oh, boy! Wish I'd lived then—adventure!" enthused Pat.

"Humph!" gram snorted. "The young never change. Right after I shot the beast, my own three wished they'd lived in the Revolution days, so's they could have had adventure shooting at the redcoats."

It was a memorable evening. Pat enjoyed the adventure of sleeping on the floor, and deplored the fact that we didn't have to sleep outdoors on the ground. . . .

## New Investments

In May we had paid in enough on the place for the agent to draw the commission, and I went to my big booming friend for my half. That $237.50 looked like a magnificent sum to me, and I didn't want it to escape me, so decided that we'd buy another place. Duncan wrote that it was ridiculous after what the first place had put me through, and that I must be a fool for punishment, and then asked slyly, "What have you found, dear? Even if it is difficult, maybe it is the right idea."

I found a place with a 100-foot frontage, with three small houses, a sort of court, with a 10,000-square-foot back yard overlooking the canyon, and an ocean view; room for more units someday. True it had not been tenanted for fourteen months, was a foreclosure and was an ugly, dirty, mustard-yellow stucco with brown trim.

I put a mortgage on my car for $150, wrote Duncan to produce $150 more. These sums, added to my commission, made up the needed $500 for down-payment and escrow charges. The purchase price was $5000. . . .

## Inventions and Ingenuity Pay Off

The renters of Acquisition 2 made me more sensitive to what was going on in the place where we lived. . . .

I have two inventors. Mr. B. is some kind of engineer, but right now works in an ice plant. Mrs. B. suffers from asthma. To help her, he invented a cylindrical affair run by electricity which purifies the air. One sad day the two wonderful dogs [that were owned by another tenant] were the concern of everybody in the place—they were desperately sick with distemper. Mrs. B. thought the ozone machine might help them. It did. Thus was opened up a market for the invention in dog-and-cat hospitals. Mr. B. went after orders in the evenings. He got so many that they didn't know how to fill them. So Mrs. B. learned how to put the machines together and made them in her apartment and typed hundreds and hundreds of letters about them. She hopes they will make enough so Mr. B. can take time out to find a new job or create his own business.

My other inventor sold hospital and doctors' equipment—X rays, and so on. His company folded. He couldn't find another job. Their money ran out. Mr. H. is a delightful man, and Mrs. H. is one of the most beautiful women in the world, movie stars not excepted. Mr. H. came to me and told me the sad truth. I told him I'd not worry too much and to stay on. He worked on an invention he had in mind. In the past he had invented several things that had been moderately successful in their day. He went out each day, job hunting, and in the evenings the two of them worked. He had a regular tool shop in the kitchen—steel files, saws, vises, hundreds of tools. Mrs. H. filed things under his direction, boiled things to test waterproofing, drilled holes in steel, and did other most amazing things. Pat, who loves to work with tools, spent most of her Sundays with them, doing all she could. She learned much and we cemented a friendship.

Their noise in the evenings got to be too much, even for one of my places, so we fixed up a work table in the laundry room. There was no way of heating it, but there they worked each night, wrapped in sweaters, sometimes until two o'clock.

The fifth month saw the thing completed to Mr. H.'s satisfaction. The sixth month saw it financed in rather a

> The depression pioneers are hard at work because capitalism in the American way is the best the world can offer.

big way and a glowing future predicted. I did not lose a dime on Mr. and Mrs. H.

Mr. and Mrs. M. discussed for weeks their peculiar capabilities, trying to decide on a course of action. Mr. M. is employed in a store at twenty-six dollars a week. They have two children, ten and fourteen years of age. Mrs. M. kept redeclaring that all she could do was cook. So they decided on a lunch counter. They found a little drive-in place, badly run down, but with usable equipment. They had $200 in their savings account. They plunged it into rent and a stock of food. Now, every evening at six he is behind the counter, helping. They make out their next day's menus after the restaurant is closed at nine. Every morning at five, Mr. M. is in the downtown markets, buying the day's supplies. At six, Mrs. M. opens the place for business. At eight, the children and their father come for breakfast, and then go off to school and work. They tell me that in six months they can open another counter, and Mr. M. will quit his job and take over the complete operation of their second lunchroom.

I could go on and on. For all I know, half the world is doing likewise. . . .

## The Benefits of Hard Work and Determination

I have now been a landlady for more than two years, and like it!

When Dunc was home last Christmas we went over all the figures in preparation for the income tax. He was surprised to find we owed only $549 besides the property payments. We'd paid more on Acquisition I than was necessary, more on Acquisition 2 than was necessary, and Acquisition 3 was doing nicely. Oh, yes, through many adventures we took on another.

We went from place to place. Dunc admired them extravagantly. He said, "Well, dear, I see you're going to make me a capitalist yet."

And that's just the idea. The depression pioneers are hard at work because capitalism in the American way is the best the world can offer.

People helped us, had faith in us, faith in the American ideal of independence. We in our turn, passed on that faith. Faith is as contagious as fear. Won't the dear Government officials please try it out sometime?

Salute the Thirty-niners!

## Note

1. "This alphabet one" refers to the New Deal, often called an alphabet soup due to all the acronyms used to stand for specific programs.

# The Civilian Conservation Corps Changes a Young Man's Life

## Robert L. Miller

In the viewpoint that follows, Robert L. Miller details the significant positive impact his participation in the Civilian Conservation Corps (CCC) had on his life. The CCC was one of the New Deal programs enacted by President Franklin D. Roosevelt in 1933 to help boost the economy by putting unemployed men to work in conservation and natural resource development. The corps was formed with dual goals—to provide employment and vocational training for young men who were out of work and to enhance and protect the natural resources of the country in aspects such as flood control, forest culture and protection, landscape and recreation, range, and wildlife. Miller explains how his participation in the program not only prevented him from falling into a

**SOURCE.** Robert L. Miller, "It's a Great Life," National Archives and Records Administration, Record Group 35, Division of Selection, "Success Stories," The Civilian Conservation Corps, 1937.

downward spiral of homelessness, dependency, and despair, but gave him a sense of self-confidence that he had not previously possessed.

There is no need to mention much of my life before I enrolled in the Civilian Conservation Corps [CCC]. It is sufficient to say that the six months previous to my enlistment were most unsatisfactory, from both a financial and mental standpoint. I was often hungry, and almost constantly broke.

When I finally enrolled in this great enterprise at Sacramento, California, in October, 1933, I was conscious of just one thing—I would be fed, clothed and sheltered during the coming winter. Also I would receive enough actual cash each month to provide the few luxuries I desired.

## Anticipation Before Arriving at the CCC

The two weeks I had to wait between the time I enrolled and the day we were to leave for camp were given over to much thinking. I began to wonder what kind of a life I was going to live for the next six months. Several questions flashed through my mind. Would I make friends with my fellow members? What kind of work would I be doing? Would I be able to "take it"? This last question was by far the most important to me.

Let me pause for a moment to give you a short character analysis of myself. For years I had been conscious of an inferiority complex that had a firm grip on me. I had tried to hide this complex beneath an outer coating of egotism. To a certain extent I had been successful—I had fooled nearly everyone but myself. Try as I may, I could not overcome the feeling that I was just a little inferior to my fellow men. I did not

> This new life [in the CCC] had a grip on me, and for the first time in months I was really happy.

Young men in the Civilian Conservation Corps got vocational training and worked to maintain and develop the nation's natural resources. **Peter Stackpole/Time & Life Pictures/Getty Images.)**

credit myself with the quality of a leader among men, but how I longed for that virtue. I had always been content to sit back and let someone else get ahead while I wished I were in his boots. It was in this frame of mind that I joined seventy other young men on the morning of

October 26, to leave for our camp in the Sierra Nevada Mountains [a mountain range running north to south in the eastern part of California].

## Settling In to the CCC Routine

Our arrival at camp that same evening was an event that I shall never forget. I was pleasantly surprised at the feeling of genuine hospitality and good cheer that existed among the older members of the company, and reached out to greet we new comers. I had expected a much different atmosphere, and I am ashamed to admit I arrived in camp with a chip on my shoulder. This feeling was soon lost in my pleasant surrounding.

Some of my self-imposed questions were answered in the first two weeks of camp life. Yes, I could make friends with my fellows, and quite easily too. Most of the friendships that I made early in my enlistment have lasted to this day. Some of those friends have left the company, others are with me now. And for those who remain, time has only strengthened the bond between us.

The second question to be answered early in the game was, could I take it? I found that I could and liked it. I could work with these boys, play with them, argue with them and hold up my end. They seemed to like me, and I knew I was fond of them.

This new life had a grip on me, and for the first time in months I was really happy. Good food, plenty of sleep, interesting work and genial companions had created quite a change—my mind was at peace.

## The Decision to Make a Change

Early in November we moved to our winter camp near Hayward, California. During the period of camp construction that followed our move, I was put in charge of several small jobs. They were insignificant in their nature, but it did me a lot of good just to think that I was considered reliable enough to boss even a small project.

These appointments started me thinking, if I could boss a small job satisfactorily, why couldn't I manage a large one? Then that old feeling would return. I would crawl in my shell and let someone else get the job I wanted and the raise in pay I coveted.

On December fifteenth several new leaders and assistant leaders were appointed. I held my breath, secretly hoping and praying I would be among the chosen ones. But as usual I was left out, just one of the many, a small cog in a large machine.

One night I went to bed rather early, rather tired after a hard days work. Something was wrong, and I didn't fall asleep right away as was my usual custom. I lay awake and thought of many things, finally dwelling on my present situation. My thoughts, when simmered down, were something like this—Here is my big chance to see if I'm going to go ahead in this world, or be just one of the crowd the rest of my life. I'm just one man in a group of two hundred young fellows, and I have just as good a chance as any of the others. So here goes, from now on I'm going to try for advancement—and I'm going to succeed. Such were my thoughts that night, for the first time I realized I had the same chance as the rest to make good.

Next morning in the light of day, things did not look so promising as I had pictured them during the night. But I now had the determination, all I needed was a starting point. In a few days I was to have my start, but it was a queer beginning.

## Taking on Leadership Roles

At various times in my life I had done a bit of wrestling, and once or twice had engaged in bouts at camp. I was asked to wrestle a boy in our camp, the bout to be a preliminary to a boxing match between our camp and a neighboring camp. I agreed, not knowing who my opponent was to be. He was not selected until the day of the fight, and when I heard his name I wanted to back out. Pride alone kept me from calling off the bout. My opponent was a huge fellow, weighing twenty-two pounds more than I, and a good three inches taller. No matter how I looked at it, I could picture only a massacre with myself on the losing end. It wasn't fear that made me want to back out, but I dreaded the thought of defeat in front of three or four hundred people.

> By enrolling in President Roosevelt's peace time army I managed to retain my self respect.

I climbed into the ring that nite a very doubtful, but determined young man. At least I would put up a good fight. When the bout was over and I emerged the victor, I knew immediately that I had made my start. I was terribly stiff and sore, but very proud and happy. Sleep did not come easily that nite. I was too excited. I kept saying to myself, "I've done it, I'm on my way." Why a physical victory should put me mentally at ease I do not know, but it did.

Then things began to happen rapidly, and soon I became convinced that I was on the right track. A group of sixteen of the most popular boys in camp were forming a club, and I was asked to become a charter member. I was only too glad to join as most of the boys in the club were either leaders or assistant leaders, and by associating with them I might learn a lot. Election of officers of the club was a prolonged affair but when it was completed, I was the president. For several days I was so excited I had a hard time controlling myself. . . .

## Achieving a Goal

A short time later news came to camp that an Educational Advisor was coming to camp to direct the boys in their pursuit of education. Also we heard that some man in camp was to be appointed to the newly created position of Assistant Educational Advisor. This new position was to carry an assistant leaders rating, which meant a raise in pay for the man lucky enough to get the Job. It wasn't long before a rumor spread through camp that three men were being considered for the new position. Imagine my surprise when I learned from a reliable source that I was one of the three.

On April 6, our Educational Advisor arrived in camp, and that evening I was told I had been appointed his assistant. My goal had been reached. I was at last one of the chosen few. Out of a group of two hundred young men I had been chosen for a position of real importance. Why, I did not know, but I felt sure there must be a reason.

Everything was made clear to me about two weeks later. One evening I was talking to our first lieutenant, he told me how it all came about. It seems the captain was aware of the year and a half I had been to college. He knew I was president of a club that had as its members most of the respected men in camp. He had studied my actions and character when I was not aware I was being watched, and he had decided I was the man for the Job. All this the lieutenant told me, much to my surprise.

In a little less than six months I had literally found myself. For twenty-two years I had doubted my right to call myself a man. My fight had been a long one, and here, in six short months I had proved to myself that I was really a man. . . .

## Lessons Learned in the CCC

I shall try to convey to you just what the Civilian Conservation Corps has meant to me. There are a great many things of which I could tell, but I shall write of only the most important. The rest I shall keep, deep down in my heart.

First of all, by enrolling in President Roosevelt's peace time army I managed to retain my self respect. I did not have to become either a parasite, living off my relatives, or a professional bum. In other words, it gave me a chance to stand on my own two feet and make my own way in the world.

Then it gave me the opportunity to make friendships that will live forever. Nine months of living in close contact with young men of my own age could hardly pass without at least a few lasting friendships. They are fine young men, those chaps who go into the forests of our country to do their bit to preserve our woods, and they are worthy of anyone's friendship. I'm very proud of the friends I've made, and if we should never meet again I can truthfully say they shall never be forgotten.

By living in close contact with these young men I learned the value of appreciating the other fellow's rights. To take one's place among his fellow men and be accepted as a friend is a fine thing for any man.

> " Thank God for President Roosevelt and his CCC. "

I had an excellent chance to develop myself physically. Many months of work in the sun have put layers of muscle on my body and turned my skin a dark tan.

But my memories, those golden thoughts that I shall keep forever, are my most valued and treasured keepsake. My album is full of pictures, each one serving as only a starting point for a long Journey into the land of happy days. Days of work in the woods, nights around the fire in the barracks, a trick played on an innocent chap, an all day hike with some of my friends, a fishing trip with one of my pals, the rush for the mess hall when the gong sounds, all of these thoughts are dear to me, and I feel sure that the next few months will bring countless more treasures with each passing day.

## The CCC Enhances Self-Confidence

These things I have mentioned are benefits derived by every young man who has been a member of the Civilian

Conservation Corps. But my personal achievement is the one glorious gift I have received from my association with the young men of the Civilian Conservation Corps.

I enrolled as a boy, unsteady, groping, unsure. I wanted something, but could not describe it or discover a means for attaining it. Then I discovered what it was I was seeking—it was the right to call myself a man. My life at camp has given me that right, and I shall be ever grateful to President Roosevelt and the CCC. Now that I am a man, with my feet firmly planted on the steps of life, I feel sure of a reasonable amount of success.

If, in my humble way I have made you realize what the Civilian Conservation Corps has done for me, I am very happy. I do not claim any honor for the change that occurred in me, it just had to be. I'm only deeply thankful that I had the chance to get acquainted with the real me.

So in parting I say "Thank God for President Roosevelt and his CCC. I shall never forget you."

# An African American Looks for Work and Finds Discrimination

### Clarence Lee

During the Great Depression, African Americans faced not only the hardships of the economic recession but also racial discrimination. They were already treated as second-class citizens, and the Depression only further demoted their status and limited their opportunities to achieve personal wealth and stability. Clarence Lee, an African American, was a teenager during the depression. When his sharecropping family could no longer support him, he was sent out to take care of himself. Lee tells in the following viewpoint about the eighteen months he spent from 1929–1931 riding in the empty freight cars of passing trains to get from one Louisiana town to another to search for work. He recounts the fear and anger he felt while riding the rails alone and tells about the anguish of encountering racial

**SOURCE.** Clarence Lee, *Riding the Rails: Teenagers on the Move During the Great Depression.* New York: TV Books, 1999. Copyright © 1999 by Errol Lincoln Ulys. All rights reserved. Republished with permission of Routledge, conveyed through Copyright Clearance Center, Inc.

discrimination at various points along his journey. His story provides a view of the dual hardships of poverty and racism that African Americans faced during the Depression.

My childhood ended the day we became share-croppers. We worked the land of a man who owned a dairy. We had to milk his cows as well as plant crops. I had pain in the ligaments of my knees and couldn't walk. My father woke me in the darkness at 3 A.M., put me on his back, and carried me to the dairy to help with the milking. For three solid months, we worked without pity or mercy.

There was no time to play like other children. I wasn't allowed to go to school. To this day I've no book learning. The kind of cropping we did was with strawberries, sweet peppers, cucumbers, and stuff like that. I was always loaded up with something.

## The Inhumanity of Sharecropping

Sharecropping was selling yourself to the devil. A Negro sharecropper had no farm equipment or farm animals. A white sharecropper often had both so that a farmer received only a third of the crop. You go in with nothing and the farmer is going to get more than a third of what you grow. To begin with, you owe money for board. If your mother wanted a little sugar or coffee, she had to go to the landowner to get it. He charged interest on every nickel.

The farmers put a mortgage on our lives. You get deeper and deeper into debt. When you can't stand one landlord any longer, you make a deal with another. He comes and pays what you owe and takes you to his place. One man sold you and another bought you like a slave. This happened over and over again. You were degraded from people down to merchandise.

You lie in bed at night on the farm, no light whatsoever, everything in total darkness. Next morning you beat the sun up and start to work. You work until the sun goes down. You are always at the mercy of someone else. Oh, yes, it was dark days—dark even at twelve noon. . . .

## Leaving Home to Ride the Rails

I wanted to stay home and fight the poverty with my family. I didn't have it in my mind to leave until my father told me, "Go fend for yourself. I cannot afford to have you around any longer." Until today it hurts when I think about it but there was nothing I could do. It was eighteen months before I saw my parents again.

We were mostly boys riding the freight trains at harvest time. You'd see some older boys with their little brothers but no fathers. Most of the time it was boys of fifteen or sixteen, teenagers like myself whose parents had put them out to make their own way. Sometimes two or three of us rode together but never a gang of youths. One or two could go and ask for help and a man might let you work in his fields. If he saw a gang of you, he didn't want you around.

It was dangerous riding the freights. You had to be careful not to stumble and fall under the wheels when you climbed on the cars. You had to jump off at the right time too 'cause once the train picked up speed you had a hard time getting off. Sometimes you slept in a boxcar

> I was nothing but dirt as far as whites were concerned.

in a rail yard; next morning when you woke up the train would be taking off with you. It was scary and dangerous but you had to do it to survive.

You never knew who was going to be on the train with you. If you hopped on a freight train with white people, you'd sit together in the boxcars. When they hit the ground they went their way and you'd go yours.

What I remember most is the "clunk" sound of the wheels hitting the joints in the track. It was a good sound and a good feeling too. "Clunk, clunk, clunk, clunk . . . " After a while you hear the whistle blow and other noises. "I'm doing OK," I'd say. "I've got a ride, I don't have to walk." You are not wandering without a purpose but going from point A to point B. You felt good 'cause you knew you were gonna get there. You were gonna try to better yourself.

## Treatment of African Americans on the Road

I came right off sharecropping into the Great Depression. On the farms I always had something to eat. Now I had nothing. There came a time when a piece of bread meant a lot to eat. There was no waste like I see today, throwing away a sandwich and so on. Many times we didn't know one day from another whether we would have food or not.

> I was motivated by poverty. I wanted to overcome it and do better in life.

Being on the road was a destructive experience for me. When I was riding the freight trains I didn't feel like an American citizen. I felt like an outcast.

I wasn't treated like a human being. I was nothing but dirt as far as whites were concerned. If you walked into a place to get a soft drink they'd kick you out. If you asked for something to eat, some would give you a piece of bread at the back door and tell you to get off the premises. Some would sic the dogs on you. It was hurtful to be treated like that. I felt very, very down.

When you went to people's houses to ask for food, if the color of your skin was white you fared better. If it was black you didn't fare too well. They might let a white man stay in the house with them, but me, I could sleep in a barn with the mules and hay.

One evening I got off a freight train and asked a farmer for work. His name was Mr. Ree. He told me I could sleep in his barn that night and he would give me something to do in the morning. So I slept in his barn and worked for him the next day.

"OK, boy, here's your pay, take it and be on your way," he said when the day was over.

And I said, "Thank you, Mr. Ree, for letting me sleep with your mules in the hay. Thank you for letting me work twelve long hours for one dollar's pay."

## Earning an Honest Living During the Depression

That's what the Depression meant to me: riding freight trains from place to place looking for something to eat. You didn't panhandle and ask for a handout but offered to work. You didn't go around stealing anything.

Once we went to a place where people were selling chickens and they gave us one. There we were, three boys with a chicken like Mr. Hoover said, but no pot![1] We picked off the feathers, pulled the intestines out, and stuffed it with mud. We dug a hole, put the chicken in the ground and made a fire above it. When the fire burned down, all we had to do was remove the dirt and we had ourselves a chicken dinner.

You wanted to buy a pair of pants or some shoes but you had nothing. I found a shoe and a boot and I wore them so long others nicknamed me "Shoeboot." You could buy second-hand shoes for forty cents, but where are you going to get the money from? You are working twelve hours a day for one dollar just to survive.

## Fear and Despair Dominate the Era

My worst fear was being shot by a farmer who didn't want me on his land. If dark hits and you were on their property, they might just shoot you. If you got to their place before dark, they might let you sleep in their barn or just tell you to keep on down the road.

I saw too many hungry people to believe that it was just me. Poverty existed all over Louisiana. Nobody had anything much. Practically everybody I met was hungry. I saw little children with bloated stomachs like those you see over in Africa.

I'd see trains coming in and going out of Baton Rouge. People were sticking on the sides or sitting in the boxcar doors with their legs hanging out. People from the country coming to the city, people from the city going to the country to look for work. Passing each other on the tracks and finding nothing when they got to their destination.

I thought the Depression would never end. I saw it was bad all over. All I could do was stay in Louisiana and try to survive doing farm work. It was the same as the sharecropping that I grew up with, only now I was getting a little pay.

## Threats of Violence

I was on a train from Baton Rouge to Denham Springs, Louisiana, going to look for work in the fields. I rode in a boxcar behind the coaches. The train was stopped at a small station along the route. I saw some people climb aboard to talk to the conductor.

After a time they left the coaches and came to the boxcar, where they looked me over real good.

"He'll have to get off," I heard the conductor say.

I asked why they wanted me off the train.

They told me that a white woman had been raped near Denham Springs. They said I fit the description, my color, my height, the way I was dressed. But they figured that I was innocent. I was in the boxcar traveling from Baton Rouge when the woman was raped. I couldn't be going and coming back at the same time.

At Denham Springs they would've ignored this. They would've taken me and lynched me.

## The Desire to Overcome Poverty

I got homesick many nights as I lay in the total darkness of a big empty barn. Sometimes I lay crying, but then I would see myself and say, "I will go on."

I was motivated by poverty. I wanted to overcome it and do better in life. I had no education, no money, no home but I had common sense. I never reached for something that was too high for me nor did I stoop to something that was so low it would drag me down.

That's what kept me going—I wanted to do better so that I could go back and help my parents and my little sister and brother.

I was doing a man's labor, not a child's labor. The work didn't get too hard and the day didn't get too long. I figured I was a man and started to think of going back home. I would be helping to put something on the table before I put my feet under the table.

### Note

1. During the 1928 presidential campaign, Herbert Hoover was quoted as saying that if he was elected he would "put a chicken in every pot"; however, the slogan was actually derived from a 1928 newspaper ad by the Republican National Committee alluding to this claim.

# The Deportation of Mexican Immigrants

## Mexican folk song, translated by Paul S. Taylor

Prior to the Great Depression, Mexican immigrants were welcomed into the United States to fill the jobs that most Americans did not want. Often, these jobs were marked by long hours of hard labor harvesting crops such as cotton, fruits, and vegetables in the fields of border states such as California, Texas, and Arizona. However, with the onset of the Depression came the scarcity of jobs, and many Americans began to seek out jobs they previously abhorred, thus displacing many Mexican migrant workers. In some cases, state legislation prohibited farms from hiring Mexican immigrants, and in extreme instances individuals who had come to the country years earlier were deported. The following viewpoint is a Mexican immigration song collected and translated by U.S. agricultural economist Paul S. Taylor, who famously traveled the country during the Depression with his wife, photographer Dorothea Lange, recording the living conditions of individuals nationwide. The song, titled "Deported [*Deportados*]" offers a glimpse into the trials of Mexican immi-

**SOURCE.** Paul S. Taylor, translator, "Deported [Deportados]," *The Era of Franklin D. Roosevelt*, 1933–1945. Edited by Richard Polenberg. Bedford/St. Martin's, 2000, pp. 221–245.

grants and the frustrations they faced in attempting to establish a better life in the United States during the Depression.

| *DEPORTADOS* | DEPORTED |
|---|---|
| *Voy á contarles, señores,* | *I am going to sing to you, señores,* |
| *voy á contarles, señores,* | *I am going to tell you, señores,* |
| *todo lo que yo sufrí* | *all about my sufferings* |
| *cuando dejé yo á mi Patria,* | *when I left my native land,* |
| *cuando dejé yo á mi Patria,* | *when I left my native land,* |
| *por venir á ese País.* | *in order to go to that country [the United States].* |
| | |
| *Serían las diez de la noche,* | *It must have been ten at night,* |
| *serían las diez de la noche* | *it must have been ten at night,* |
| *comenzó un tren á silvar;* | *when a train began to whistle;* |
| *oí que dijo mi madre* | *I heard my mother say,* |
| *hay viene ese tren ingrato* | *"Here comes that hateful train* |
| *que á mi hijo se va á llevar.* | *to take my son away."* |
| | |
| *Por fin sonó la campana,* | *Finally they rang the bell,* |
| *por fin sonó la campana;* | *finally they rang the bell.* |
| *vámonos de la estación,* | *"Let's go on out of the station;* |
| *no quiero ver á mi madre* | *I'd rather not see my mother* |
| *llorar por su hijo querido,* | *weeping for her dear son,* |
| *por su hijo del corazón,* | *the darling of her heart."* |
| | |
| *Cuando á Chihuahua llegamos,* | *When we reached Chihuahua,[1]* |
| *cuando á Chihuahua llegamos,* | *when we reached Chihuahua,* |
| *se notó gran confusión,* | *there was great confusion:* |
| *los empleados de la aduana,* | *the customs house employees,* |
| *los empleados de la aduana* | *the customs house employees,* |
| *que pasaban revisión.* | *were having an inspection.* |
| | |
| *Llegamos por fin á Juárez,* | *We finally arrived at Juárez,[2]* |
| *llegamos por fin á Juárez* | *we finally arrived at Juárez,* |

| | |
|---|---|
| *ahí fué mi apuración* | where I had my inspection: |
| *que dónde va, que dónde viene* | "Where are you going, where are you from, |
| | |
| *cuánto dinero tiene* | how much money have you |
| *para entrar á esta nación* | in order to enter this country?" |
| | |
| *Señores, traigo dinero,* | "Gentlemen, I have money, |
| *señores, traigo dinero* | gentlemen, I have money |
| *para poder emigrar,* | enough to be able to emigrate." |
| *su dinero nada vale,* | "Your money is worthless, |
| *su dinero nada vale,* | your money is worthless; |
| *te tenemos que bañar.* | we'll have to give you a bath." |
| | |
| *Los güeros son muy maloras,* | The "blondes" [Americans] are very unkind; |
| | |
| *los gringos son muy maloras,* | the gringos [Spanish slang to refer to Americans] are very unkind. |
| | |
| *se valen de la ocasión,* | They take advantage of the chance |
| *y á todos los mexicanos,* | to treat all the Mexicans, |
| *y á todos los mexicanos,* | to treat all the Mexicans |
| *nos tratan sin compasión.* | without compassion. |
| | |
| *Hoy traen la gran polvadera,* | Today they are rounding them up, |
| *hoy traen la gran polvadera* | today they are rounding them up; |
| *y sin consideración,* | and without consideration |
| *mujeres niños y ancianos* | women, children, and old folks |
| *los llevan á la frontera* | are taken to the frontier |
| *los echan de esa nación,* | and expelled from that country. |
| | |
| *Adiós, paisanos queridos,* | So farewell, dear countrymen, |
| *adiós, paisanos queridos,* | so farewell, dear countrymen; |
| *ya nos van á deportar* | they are going to deport us now, |
| *pero no somos bandidos* | but we are not bandits, |
| *pero no somos bandidos* | but we are not bandits, |
| *venimos á camellar.* | we came to camellar.[3] |

Workers from Mexico often performed agricultural labor during the Depression, but also became targets of a deportation program intended to preserve such jobs for U.S. citizens. (**AP Images.**)

| | |
|---|---|
| *Los espero allá en mi tierra,* | *I'll wait for you there in my country,* |
| *los espero allá en mi tierra,* | *I'll wait for you there in my country* |
| *ya no hay más revolución;* | *now that there is no revolution;* |
| *vamonos cuates queridos* | *let us go, brothers dear,* |
| *seremos bien recibidos* | *we will be well received* |
| *en nuestra bella nación.* | *in our own beautiful land.* |

## Notes

1. Chihuahua is the name of a Mexican state bordering the United States; it is also the name of that state's capital.
2. Juárez is the largest border city in the Mexican state of Chihuahua, across the Rio Grande river from El Paso, Texas.
3. This word appears in Spanish in the translated version because the translator could not find a word that meant the equivalent in English; Paul S. Taylor translated the word to mean, "to work like a beast of burden, humped over like a camel."

# CHRONOLOGY

**1792**   The New York Stock Exchange (NYSE) is founded.

**1817**   Members of the NYSE draft a constitution and officially name the organization the New York Stock Exchange and Board. The name is shortened to the New York Stock Exchange in 1863.

**1914**   The NYSE closes briefly following the start of World War I. In November, it reopens only to trade bonds to aid the war effort, but opens fully for stock trading by mid-December.

**1918**   World War I ends.

**1920**   A post-war recession begins in January but ends 18 months later in July 1921.

**1921**   The United States begins a period of economic prosperity following the end of the 1921 recession. Economic growth and prosperity will continue through the end of the decade with increased consumer spending, expansion of the stock market, and full employment.

**1928**   November 6: Herbert Hoover is elected president of the United States.

**1929**   September 3: Stock prices of the Dow Jones Industrial Average peak and immediately begin to fall the following day.

October 24: Stock prices reach a historic low with 12.9

million shares traded; Wall Street bankers attempt to halt the free fall and stabilize the market by pooling their money and purchasing a large quantity of "blue chip" stocks. The stability provided is only temporary and this day comes to be known as Black Thursday.

October 28: The stock market falls another 13%. This day is referred to as Black Monday.

October 29: 16 million stocks are traded and $14 billion is lost on the stock market. "Black Tuesday" sets a record low for the stock market to this point and ignites a nationwide panic.

President Hoover signs the Agricultural Marketing Act hoping to halt the deflation of crop prices by purchasing surplus crops and providing monetary aid to farm organizations.

The Mexican Repatriation program begins with Hoover's authorization. Mexicans and Mexican Americans go to Mexico both voluntarily and involuntarily due to high unemployment rates, threats of deportation, and enticement by both the U.S. and Mexican governments. By 1937, estimates of the number of individuals displaced reach nearly half a million.

1930    Summer: The Great Plains region of the United States experiences the beginning of a prolonged period of dust storms caused by a combination of drought and poor farming techniques that erode the region's soil. The area most affected is called the Dust Bowl and includes parts of Colorado, Kansas, Iowa, Oklahoma, and Texas.

June 17: President Hoover signs the Smoot-Hawley Tariff Act, which raises tariffs on goods imported to the United States.

December 10: A crowd of around 25,000 people descends on the Southern Boulevard branch of the Bank of the United States located in the Bronx, New York. Depositors withdraw $2 million dollars.

December 11: The Bank of the United States closes. Though not the first bank to close, this bank's closure is seen as the tipping point that led to widespread bank failure.

**1931**    June 30: President Hoover calls for a freeze to Germany's reparation payments to France and Allied repayment of war debt to the United States.

**1932**    June 17: The "Bonus Army," made up of thousands of World War I veterans and their families, convenes in Washington, D.C. and demands the early payment of the bonus they would be able to claim in 1945 under the Adjusted Service Certificate Law.

July 28: Washington, D.C. police attempt to expel the Bonus Army and end up shooting and killing two veterans. The U.S. Army charges the camp, killing several more and wounding hundreds.

November 8: Franklin D. Roosevelt is elected president of the United States.

**1933**    The U.S. unemployment rate reaches a high of 24.9%.

March 5: President Roosevelt declares a national bank holiday, forcing all banks to close for four days.

March 9: The Emergency Banking Act passes Congress and is signed into law. It authorizes government oversight of bank reopenings and the advance of federal loans to banks in need.

May 12: The Agricultural Adjustment Act is passed. The legislation seeks to raise the price of crops by reducing agricultural surplus. To do so, farmers are paid to use less land and plant fewer crops.

May 18: The Tennessee Valley Authority (TVA) is created to provide affordable power to rural communities in the Tennessee Valley region. The TVA also aids in flood control, manufacture of fertilizer, and economic development.

June 16: The National Industrial Recovery Act passes. In an attempt to stimulate economic recovery, Title I gives the president the authority to regulate industry and allow price-fixing. Title II creates the Public Works Administration, which seeks to employ Americans in the construction of public projects, increase consumer spending, stabilize the economy, and spur the regeneration of U.S. industry.

The Glass-Steagall Act separates banking by purpose into commercial and investment. It also founds the Federal Deposit Insurance Corporation (FDIC), which insures Americans' deposits in member banks.

1934    June 6: The U.S. Securities and Exchange Commission (SEC) is established. The SEC is charged with regulating the stock market as well as the companies and brokers selling shares.

1935    April 8: The Works Progress Administration—renamed the Works Projects Administration (WPA) in 1939—is founded under a presidential order. During its eight year existence, the WPA creates 8 million jobs including projects as varied as highway construction, drama production, and park building.

April 14: The Social Security Act is passed. Provisions of the act include financial aid and insurance for the elderly, unemployed, impoverished, widowed, and orphaned.

**1936** November 3: Incumbent candidate Franklin D. Roosevelt is elected to a second term as president.

**1937** Mid-year, the recovering U.S. economy falters. For the next 13 months, the steady economic improvements that had characterized the Roosevelt presidency to this point drastically reverse with industrial production falling 30% and an increase in unemployment from 14.3% in the early part of the year to 19% in 1938.

**1938** February 10: The Federal National Mortgage Association, known commonly as Fannie Mae, is created to aid low-income families in obtaining mortgages.

February 16: Congress passes legislation to create the Federal Crop Insurance Corporation (FCIC), which provides crop insurance to protect American farmers and agricultural corporations against extreme weather conditions that could limit crop production.

**1940** November 5: On the brink of U.S. entry into World War II, Franklin D. Roosevelt wins an unprecedented third presidential election.

**1941** The United States enters World War II; the unemployment rate falls below 10%.

# FOR FURTHER READING

**Books**

Frederick Lewis Allen, *Since Yesterday: The 1930's in America, September 3, 1929–September 3, 1939*. New York: Perennial Library, 1986.

Jonathan Alter, *The Defining Moment: FDR's Hundred Days and the Triumph of Hope*. New York: Simon & Schuster, 2006.

Caroline Bird, *Invisible Scar: The Great Depression, and What It Did to American Life, from Then Until Now*. New York: Pocket Books, 1966.

Conrad Black, *Franklin Delano Roosevelt: Champion of Freedom*. New York: Public Affairs, 2003.

Michael L. Cooper, *Dust to Eat: Drought and the Depression in the 1930's*. New York: Clarion, 2004.

Morris Dickstein, *Dancing in the Dark: A Cultural History of the Great Depression*. New York: Norton, 2009.

Ronald Edsforth, *The New Deal: America's Response to the Great Depression*. Malden, MA: Blackwell, 2000.

Glen H. Elder, *Children of the Great Depression: Social Change in Life Experience*. Chicago: University of Chicago Press, 1974.

Burton W. Folsom, *New Deal or Raw Deal?: How FDR's Economic Legacy Has Damaged America*. New York: Threshold Editions, 2008.

Vincent H. Gaddis, *Herbert Hoover, Unemployment, and the Public Sphere: A Conceptual History, 1919–1933*. Lanham, MD: University Press of America, 2005.

Philip Hanson, *This Side of Despair: How the Movies and American Life Intersected during the Great Depression*. Madison, NJ: Fairleigh Dickinson University Press, 2008.

David E. Kyvig, *Daily Life in the United States, 1920–1940: How Americans Lived through the "Roaring Twenties" and the Great Depression*. Chicago: Ivan R. Dee, 2004.

Bruce Lenthall, *Radio's America: The Great Depression and the Rise of Modern Mass Culture*. Chicago: University of Chicago Press, 2007.

Neil M. Maher, *Nature's New Deal: The Civilian Conservation Corps and the Roots of the American Environmental Movement*. New York: Oxford University Press, 2008.

James R. McGovern, *And a Time for Hope: Americans in the Great Depression*. Westport, CT: Praeger, 2000.

Andrew J.F. Morris, *The Limits of Voluntarism: Charity and Welfare from the New Deal through the Great Society*. New York: Cambridge University Press, 2009.

Jim Powell, *FDR's Folly: How Roosevelt and his New Deal Prolonged the Great Depression*. New York: Crown Forum, 2003.

Eric Rauchway, *The Great Depression & the New Deal: A Very Short Introduction*. New York: Oxford University Press, 2008.

Elliot A. Rosen, *Roosevelt, the Great Depression, and the Economics of Recovery*. Charlottesville, VA: University of Virginia Press, 2005.

Gene Smiley, *Rethinking the Great Depression*. Chicago: I.R. Dee, 2002.

Jean Edward Smith, *FDR*. New York: Random House, 2007.

Studs Terkel, *Hard Times: An Oral History of the Great Depression*. New York: New Press, 2000.

Timothy Walch, ed., *Uncommon Americans: The Lives and Legacies of Herbert and Lou Henry Hoover*. Westport, CT: Praeger, 2003.

T.H. Watkins, *The Hungry Years: A Narrative History of the Great Depression in America*. New York: Henry Holt & Co., 1999.

## Periodicals

Jerry Askeroth, "In Hindsight, Blame Hitler or Hoover for Hard Times," *Insight on the News*, April 16, 2001.

Kevin Baker, "Barack Hoover Obama," *Harper's*, July 2009.

Randy Barrett, "Depression Comparisons Fall Flat," *National Journal*, April 4, 2009.

H.W. Brands, "15 Minutes that Saved America," *American History*, October 2008.

Alan Brinkley, "No Deal," *New Republic*, December 31, 2008.

John S. Brown, "The U.S. Army and the Great Depression," *Army*, December 2008.

Clive Crook, "Protectionism and the Stimulus," *National Journal*, February 7, 2009.

Ivan Dmitri, "No Jobs in California," *Saturday Evening Post*, November 12, 1938.

*The Economist*, "The Battle of Smoot-Hawley," December 20, 2008.

*The Economist*, "The Lessons of 1937," June 20, 2009.

Edwin F. Gay, "The Great Depression," *Foreign Affairs*, July 1932.

John Steele Gordon, "The Man Who Wasn't There," *American Heritage*, November 1991.

Elliot J. Gorn, "The Meanings of Depression-Era Culture," *Chronicle of Higher Education*, June 26, 2009.

William Gropper, "The Dust Bowl," *Nation*, August 21, 1937.

William Howarth and Chris Johns, "The Okies: Beyond the Dust Bowl," *National Geographic*, September 1984.

Will Manley, "The Manley Arts: A Child of the Depression," *Booklist*, March 1, 2009.

Matthew McClearn, "Name that Recession," *Canadian Business*, September 28, 2009.

H.I. Phillips, "Never Again in the Stock Market!" *Saturday Evening Post*, December 28, 1935.

Robert J. Samuelson, "What We Learn from the 1920s," *Newsweek*, February 12, 2001.

Charles Scaliger, "The Great Depression," *New American*, June 23, 2008.

Lois Spear, "Hard Times, "*America*, June 8, 2009.

Richard L. Strout, "Mr. Hoover as a Terrapin Progressive," *New Republic*, March 16, 1959.

Studs Terkel, "When Times Were Really Hard," *Atlantic*, April 1970.

Marianna Torgovnick, "The Buoyancy of Depression Entertainment," *Chronicle of Higher Education*, April 3, 2009.

Andrew B. Wilson, "Five Myths About the Great Depression," *Wall Street Journal*, November 4, 2008.

## Web Sites

**America in the 1930s (http://xroads.virginia.edu/~1930s/front.html).** At this Web site, visitors can explore the decade of the Great Depression through cultural artifacts such as film, newspaper clips, art, and radio broadcasts.

**Digital History (www.digitalhistory.uh.edu).** This Web site combines primary and secondary source documents to offer a complete history of the United States, including a section on the Great Depression. The site contains an online textbook, links to outside, approved Web sites, and a timeline of important events.

**New Deal Network (http://newdeal.feri.org).** This Web site offers a comprehensive guide to the events, people, projects, and legislation of the Great Depression through primary source documents, photographs, and links to other archival sites.

**Voices from the Dust Bowl (http://lcweb2.loc.gov/ammem/afctshtml/tshome.html).** This Library of Congress Web site serves as a clearinghouse for documents related to the experience of migrant workers who moved to California to work at the large Farm Security Administration work camps during the waning years of the Great Depression. Documents on the site include audio recordings, photographs, texts, and transcripts of songs.

**Wessels Living History Farm (www.livinghistoryfarm.org).** This Web site of Wessels Living History Farm located in York, Nebraska, is dedicated, along with the farm, to providing information about the history of farming in the United States. The site is divided into sections by decade and provides video interviews with individuals who lived as farmers during the 1920s and 1930s, as well as additional historical information about the periods.

# INDEX